W9-BST-901

# BOAT MAINTENANCE

## The Essential Guide
## to Cleaning, Painting, and Cosmetics

## Bill Burr

**International Marine / McGraw-Hill**

Camden, Maine • New York • San Francisco • Washington, D.C. • Auckland •
Bogotá • Caracas • Lisbon • London • Madrid • Mexico City • Milan • Montreal •
New Delhi • San Juan • Singapore • Sydney • Tokyo • Toronto

## International Marine

*A Division of The McGraw·Hill Companies*

10 9 8 7 6 5 4 3 2

Copyright © 2000 William M. Burr
All rights reserved. The publisher takes no responsibility for the use of any
of the materials or methods described in this book, nor for the products thereof.
The name "International Marine" and the International Marine logo are trademarks of The McGraw-Hill Companies. Printed in the United States of America.

*Library of Congress Cataloging-in-Publication Data*
Burr, William M.
    Boat Maintenance : the essential guide to cleaning, painting, and cosmetics /
Bill Burr.
        p.    cm.
    Includes index.
    ISBN 0-07-135703-3 (alk. paper)
    1. Boats and boating—Maintenance and repair. I. Title.
    VM321.B965 2000
    623.8'202'0288—dc21                                    00-022834

Questions regarding the content of this book should be addressed to
International Marine
P.O. Box 220
Camden, ME  04843
http://www.internationalmarine.com

Questions regarding the ordering of this book should be addressed to
The McGraw-Hill Companies
Customer Service Department
P.O. Box 547
Blacklick, OH  43004
Retail customers: 1-800-262-4729
Bookstores: 1-800-722-4726

This book is printed on 60# Finch Opaque.

Printed by R. R. Donnelley, Crawfordsville, IN
Design by Shannon Thomas
Production management by Janet Robbins
Page layout by PD&PS
Edited by Jon Eaton, Alex Barnett, and John Vigor

The author and publisher have made all effort to reproduce registered trademarks correctly.

**WARNING:** Repairing and maintaining your boat can expose you to potentially dangerous situations. Reference to brand names does not indicate endorsement of or guarantee
the safety of using these products. In using this book, the reader releases the author, publisher, and distributor from liability for any loss or injury, including death, allegedly caused, in
whole or in part, by relying on information contained in this book.

IT IS IMPOSSIBLE TO ENJOY IDLING THOROUGHLY
UNLESS ONE HAS PLENTY OF WORK TO DO.

—Jerome K. Jerome, *On Being Idle*, 1886

With great humility, the author wishes to thank David Brown, Mike Kennedy, Keith Irwing, Roger Siminoff, Doug Templin, Neil Wilson, and the hundreds of other experts who added their ideas to this book. Thanks to Tom Calabrese and Bob Hopkins at Millennium Inorganic Chemicals, who put together the astonishing electron photographs. At International Marine, thanks to Jon Eaton, Alex Barnett, and John Vigor for some superb editing.

# Contents

# INTRODUCTION

After a long professional career in the chemical industry, I retired, bought a 37-foot sailboat, and moved aboard. The boat was 14 years old and in pretty good shape for its age, but now that it was my home and my path to adventure and freedom, I wanted it to be perfect. As a liveaboard, I found every little nick and noisy drip. It was soon obvious that the previous owner had done superficial maintenance at best. The toilet leaked from some inaccessible dark place my hand could barely reach. The cooling-pump impeller failed on my first trip. Lockers and lazarettes smelled like mushrooms in a dank cellar. There were rust marks and bird droppings on the white deck. Scratches marred the interior teak. The bilge was a mystery of damp hairballs and dark stains. Yet, I already loved the boat, and like all suitors, I made it a promise that it would soon be the best-looking boat on the bay.

Six months later, it was complimented by almost everyone who passed by. We had been through a winter together. I had new confidence in it because I had been in every corner, in every crevice, and under every closed compartment. I had seen its innards and restored it inside and out. It was a proud beauty once again.

But, in order to transform it, I had to learn how to clean and polish, how to choose between repair and replacement. A boat requires preventive maintenance like few other properties. It simply must be done. Like most who come to boats, I didn't automatically know how to clean and fix everything. I had to figure it out the hard way, learning through the tedious process of scrubbing, polishing, tightening, and repairing without any clear idea of what I was doing. When I began, I bought a deck-cleaning soap. It worked okay. Then someone told me about a biodegradable detergent called SUDBURY BOAT ZOAP. It was remarkably better. Next, I scrubbed at the tar and sea-gunk fouling my fenders. They had seen years of abuse and were so unsightly that I considered replacing them before my reputation was ruined. The marine store recommended a popular fender cleaner. It did no more than smear the mess and ruin a good rag. Through trial and error, I finally discovered a tar remover in an automotive store that cleaned the fenders in minutes. On and on it went. Reading labels was almost useless. Most manufacturers gave no clue to the composition of their cleaning compounds apart from a warning when they contained toxic ingredients. Selection was pure chance. I never knew if I was using the best product or the worst. I found that high-priced marine products for cleaning, polishing, and renewing were often no better than supermarket staples such as FANTASTIK and WINDEX. On the other hand, I discovered some marine compounds that did what they promised and more. WEST HEAD LUBE, for example, made my finicky toilet pump work like new.

In the course of bringing my boat back to civility, I devoured books on maintenance. Cleaning and refurbishing occasionally came up but were treated as lightweight subjects compared to engine repair or rewiring. In vain I searched for answers to my long list of problems—nicks in the teak, scratches in the Lexan, mildewed fabric, faded woodwork, the chaos of the bilge. I found some solutions in the popular boating books, but almost never recommendations for specific products. Most boat owners search the shelves at marine stores for nonexistent clues to the best product. As I did, they learn through trial and error, wasting time and money. Finding the right product was just as frustrating for me, but with my background in chemistry, I took it further. The result is this book.

Anyone with the desire, strong arms, *Boat Maintenance,* and some time can turn an "also-ran" vessel into a dream boat. This book will tell you how to turn an ordinary boat into the pride of the anchorage. Five chapters deal with specific surfaces requiring cleaning: fiberglass, wood, metal, fabric, and plastics. Chapter 5 explains in layman's terms the complex and sometimes baffling world of paints, varnishes, and other coatings. Chapter 6 delves into the mysteries of sealants and adhesives. Chapter 9 covers the interior of the boat. At the end of each chapter, you will find a quick-reference chart summarizing key points.

Appendix 1 contains extensive preventive maintenance schedules. A boat's parts need maintenance, periodic adjustment, and occasional replacement. The older the boat, the more often it should be inspected. By following a regular cleaning schedule and keeping a spotless boat, most repairs and replacements can be delayed indefinitely. Equally important, scheduled maintenance puts your hands on every inch of the boat methodically and religiously. Potential disasters are discovered early. In the long run, your boat will cost less to run and be safer to operate. In appendix 1, you will find weekly, monthly, seasonal, and annual to-do lists. The appendix also contains a list of items to check every time you leave the dock, and another list of reminders to follow before leaving the boat after every outing.

Three more appendixes provide answers to specific cleaning questions. Appendix 2 identifies typical maintenance problems. Appendix 3 lists specific boat areas and associated projects. Appendix 4 lists common chemicals and identifies corresponding brand-name cleaning compounds. Finally, the product index identifies some 150 brand-name products and their generic equivalents, and the general index gives you yet another way into the text.

The organization of the appendixes will allow you to answer a maintenance question however you approach it. Suppose you need to clean a stainless-steel fitting. You might turn to appendix 2, Individual Maintenance Tasks, look under stainless, and be directed to the page in the Metal chapter where stainless-steel corrosion is addressed. Appendix 3, Cleaning and Maintanance Projects, contains a section on deck care that refers you to the page that covers stainless-steel deck hardware. Finally, if you want to know what chemicals are in stainless cleaners, look in appendix 4, Chemical Ingredients. The product index will suggest NOXON 7, FLITZ, and NEVR-DULL for polishing stainless steel.

I have suggested many home remedies, some as simple as using cold water to remove blood stains from sailcloth, lemon and salt to clean brass, or diapers to sop up oil from the engine well. I can't stress enough that the best, least expensive, and most readily available cleaner is water. Owners of well-maintained boats religiously wash down with freshwater after every trip. It is no accident that water is called the universal solvent. It's often the safest and most effective cleaner available, though we tend to overlook it in the frenzied and expensive search for the magic cure.

One of my favorite curatives is WINDEX, the common household window cleaner. It's the closest thing to the perfect cleaning product I know. If it's used while a stain is still wet, it will remove blood, soft drinks, salt, tobacco stains, and almost all other water-soluble catastrophes. The alcohol and ammonia in it remove most grease stains and also act as a disinfectant. It may be used with confidence on cushions, varnished areas, vinyl headers, and skid-proof surfaces. I've found almost no wet stain that it doesn't clean.

Have you noticed the rust that occurs where PVC tubes cover standing rigging? Beneath these anti-chafe tubes, a slow and deadly deterioration of wire takes place. In the dark, damp confines of this environment, mildew and moisture are at work. You need to stop this corrosion as soon as possible. The Metal chapter suggests sliding the tubes up, taping them in place, and then wiping the wire down with CLOROX or lacquer thinner, which leaves no residue when it dries. You then scrub with coarse bronze wool as necessary, but *never* with steel wool, as steel wool leaves powdered iron specks that rust wherever they fall. If corrosion is visible on the wire, wipe a generous amount of **WD-40** on the wire before the tubes are let back down into place. Finish by flushing the deck with water to remove any bronze wool residue. This is an example of a short maintenance job that should be repeated twice a year.

## A Note on Product Names

In text and in tables, we've used a special typeface to help you identifiy brand-name products. The bolded PRODUCT NAME STYLE allows you to distinguish between a brand-name product and a generic name for something. Think KLEENEX versus facial tissue. The product index, which begins on page 159, gives the full brand name for each product, as well as its generic equivalent. We've made an effort to give current product names, but bear in mind that manufacturers continually change, repackage, and rename products. What's on your local marine or hardware store shelf might be newer than a specific product indentified here—or it might be older, for that matter.

In part, this book is a summary of the hundreds of informal interviews I have conducted with boaters who have tried every conceivable product during their own years of trial and error. *Boat Maintenance* passes their combined wisdom on to you. Some of the suggestions were solicited from charter operators who must keep their boats in spotless condition week after week. Others were garnered from interviews with marine engineers, marina operators, boat manufacturers, marine supply store employees, and pleasure-boat owners. If you follow their advice, you will never again have to stand in the aisle of the marine supply store, baffled by the vast array of choices. You will be able to select with confidence a product recommended by your peers. This, in essence, is what *Boat Maintenance* is: a record of products and techniques compiled by people who, like you, have tried and tested and finally found products they swear by.

Very few product labels disclose what chemicals are contained in the bottle; instead, they proudly announce how easy the brand is to use and the marvels it works. Knowing which chemicals a product contains helps environmentally concerned boaters avoid cleaning compounds that still use harmful ingredients such as phosphates. A quick search in appendix 4, Chemical Ingredients, will answer this concern.

A modern pleasure boat is an assemblage of plastic, wood, and metal, a masterpiece of design made strong enough to withstand all that nature can dish out, a thing so beautiful that it inspires poems, so delicate in form that it is still addressed as "she." Has any other inanimate object created so many dreams of adventure? Boats have been called aphrodisiacs and vehicles to another life. When the wind and sun are perfect, when beauty, grace, and escapism combine, it is still efficiency, skill, prudence, and care that make everything work. Without them, the beauty and the dreams are lost. Without care, even love dies. Laying hands on every inch of a boat's woodwork, fiberglass, and metal is the best way to know it, the way to keep it young and beautiful. In the end, *Boat Maintenance* is about prolonging the romance between you and your boat.

# 1

# GENERAL CARE

This chapter provides an overview of cleaning and cosmetics: the chemistry behind cleaning agents; the three basic steps of any cleaning and maintenance project; the cleaning supplies and clothing you'll need; the importance of regular housekeeping; and environmental concerns. But first, leaving aside aesthetics for the moment, consider the economic implications of not doing preventive maintenance.

Failure to replace a $25 impeller on a regular basis might lead to overheating. If the engine is not shut down immediately, a simple problem could result in an engine rebuild costing thousands of dollars. Simply by washing down a winch after every sail, you will prevent salt buildup, which, if unchecked, can lead to failure and an overhaul requiring a $20 winch kit. By spraying a $10 corrosion inhibitor on lifeline connections, turnbuckles, and battery terminals, you can prevent corrosion damage that would cost hundreds of dollars in replacement fittings and batteries. By routinely touching up varnished surfaces, you will postpone or avoid the endless hours of labor involved in scraping off the old varnish and applying six or seven coats of new. The costs in labor and materials in these examples are merely the tip of the iceberg if preventive maintenance is neglected. Preventing problems will be a central theme of this book.

Almost all maintenance jobs can be categorized as mild, moderate, or severe. It doesn't require much expertise to determine how advanced the damage is—it will be all too obvious to the eye. The secret is not to let a maintenance problem go beyond the *mild* category. Once the job becomes moderate or severe, the amount of time, money, and effort increases exponentially.

Cosmetic care of a boat can be enjoyable and rewarding, or it can be a nightmare. Think about what should be done. Schedule the job so that it happens. If you plan ahead, you're more likely to spend your time and money wisely. Cleaning is one of the easiest of boat projects and one that gives great satisfaction.

A West Coast Perspective

# A West Coast Perspective

**Roger Siminoff** has been boating for nearly 40 years. After serving as national sales manager for Loran and GPS at Trimble Navigation, he created Boatdoktor, a company performing repair and maintenance services for boaters in the San Francisco Bay area. In 1993, he designed the marine navigation system for the film *Waterworld*. He has written the popular *Boating 101* (International Marine, 1999), and articles for *Yachting* magazine. A color graphics developer, he sails a 33-foot Pearson in the San Francisco area. Since Roger has boated extensively on both coasts and in the Caribbean, I asked him how boat care and maintenance on the West Coast compared with other parts of the country:

## Climate

"Probably the most obvious and significant difference is the weather. Boats moored in the San Francisco Bay area experience little humidity and a rainless summer. Except for marinas along the San Francisco waterfront, the mean daytime temperature is 75°F from March to October. Evenings are cool, and likewise low in humidity. Rain in the winter months is abbreviated, and the rain is quite clean compared to the acid rain of the East Coast, and leaves little residue on the boats. The Seattle area receives far more rain, but it is also clean; the San Diego region gets far less than either. West Coast sea temperatures hover around the 55°F mark all year. The cold wind tends to inhibit mildew, and the cold water helps keep bottom paint from fouling as quickly as it does in the higher water temperatures along the East Coast. In many ways, this is a more forgiving climate."

## Anchoring and Docking

"Most marinas along the West Coast feature slips and docks. Mooring out, which is so common in the East, is rarely found in the West. As far as maintenance is concerned, slips have a great advantage in that they provide a solid platform for cleaning hulls and topsides. But they are also an obstacle to hit when docking. All it takes is a little bump to mark the gelcoat or paint. It's a good idea to protect the topsides by covering the fenders with some form of cloth protective sleeve. Many of these are on the market.

"West Coast slips usually have fresh water available for frequently hosing down. Removing dried salt is one of the best ways to keep teak, gelcoat, and stainless steel or aluminum fittings bright and shiny. Hose down boats after every use; if you keep your boat in an industrial area or near an airport, rinse it down between outings.

"Most slips also have shore power. As convenient as this is, it can present some serious maintenance problems. Some marina power lines may be improperly wired or improperly grounded. This can lead to a rapid erosion of boat parts due to electrolysis. More importantly, there can be a serious shock hazard. All vessels connected to shore power should be fitted with ground-fault interrupters."

## Exterior Woodwork

"The dry heat of the West Coast is not especially friendly to oil finishes on teak. It causes them to dry sooner than desired. Varnishes quickly become brittle and cloudy. Out here, most of the teak finishes on the market need to be touched up annually and completely stripped off every two to three years. One exception is **SIKKENS CETOL**, which seems to hold its color and brightness well in the California sun. **CETOL** requires only a mild wet-sanding and a new refresher top coat. By the way, wet-sanding is a great way to improve the surface of any finished wood. You need a bowl of water and wet-or-dry sandpaper, which typically has a black backing. Keep the paper wet by dunking it in the bowl between each use. Sand the coated finish with the wetted paper. The water keeps the sandpaper from clogging and keeps the finish cool. Dry the excess water off the wood. Let it stand until dry and apply your next coat of finish. You'll be surprised at the result."

There seems to be something about boats that makes new boaters doubt their knowledge and competence in regard to maintenance, cleaning, and repair. There is no reason to be afraid of your boat. The surfaces and parts you'll be working on are, in most ways, similar to those you are familiar with on the car and at home. Refer to that experience to get started.

You may not be able to do it all. You may decide a given maintenance project is just too difficult or time-consuming, and is best left to a professional. A bad case of osmotic blisters requires elaborate preparation of the surface, the application of multiple coats of a barrier coat, and, finally, antifouling paint. If you do hire a professional, observe how they do the job, and what tools they use. But don't automatically call one when the job looks tough. First, talk to other boaters, and refer to the appropriate subject in this book.

In the chapters that follow, there are references to some 150 brand-name products. Each one has been included either because of my own experience or because it was consistently recommended by the boaters and marine professionals I interviewed. There has been no compensation in any form for any product recommendation. There are many similar products on the market that are not included, either because I haven't used them or because they were not recommended as often. Nevertheless, such products may also work well. The fact that a product is not recommended in the book doesn't mean that I have tried it and rejected it. There surely are products we haven't even heard of that would do a fine job.

# The Chemistry of Cleaning

A few generalizations about the chemistry of cleaners are worth making at the outset. One of the determining factors in choosing a cleaner is the pH (the degree of acidity or alkalinity) of the product. A scale has been established to classify the pH of chemicals. The scale runs from 1 (acid) to 14 (alkaline) with neutral products in the center at the number 7.

| Acid | | | | | | Neutral | | | | | | | Alkaline |
|---|---|---|---|---|---|---|---|---|---|---|---|---|---|
| I | 2 | 3 | 4 | 5 | 6 | 7 | 8 | 9 | I0 | II | I2 | I3 | I4 |

On the left side of the pH scale are the *acid* ingredients, such as oxalic, phosphoric, and hydrochloric acid, which, depending on their strength, run from 1 up to the neutral value of 7. The *alkaline* ingredients, such as chlorine (bleach), ammonia, and sodium hypochlorite, fall between 7 and 14. The closer an acid gets to 1, the stronger its effect will be—and the more hazardous it is to a user. Likewise, the closer an alkali gets to 14, the stronger and more hazardous it becomes. Neutral, again, is in the middle, at a pH near 7.

A strong rust and stain remover like ON & OFF, which contains three different acids, will have a low pH and should be applied only with protective gloves and glasses. A mild cleaner like BOAT ZOAP will fall into the neutral pH category. A degreaser will be on the alkaline side (see below) and, like an acid, should also be used with protective gloves and glasses.

Most household cleaners contain strong alkaline ingredients (such as lye or sodium hypochlorite) for their grease-cutting properties. They are intended for use on surfaces like Formica and vinyl, and in general are too harsh for surfaces on the boat such as gelcoat. In addition, alkaline cleaners should not be allowed to dry in place and are subject to sunlight degradation outdoors. If you let alkaline household cleaners dry on fiberglass, they may etch the surface. Rinse them off before they have a chance to dry. On the boat, you may well be cleaning a large surface area in direct sunlight without easy access to freshwater for rinsing, so be very careful.

Most of the high-powered stain cleaners like ON & OFF contain acids. In the marine environment, acidic cleaners are most effective on rust and waterline stains. Acidic cleaners don't have much effect on grime and oil.

In summary, many specialized boat cleaners have a pH value near neutral to avoid the hazards associated with high acid or alkali content. Some are distinctly acidic to remove rust and stains, and some are alkaline for cutting grease. Read the product labels and try to determine the specific intent of a product. Don't just grab any cleaner at will. Many marine cleaners are concentrated and should be diluted with water before use— don't just pour the cleaner on a rag and wipe away. Again, read the label and follow the instructions. Quite often, a cleaner will do a better job if it's left on the surface for a few minutes, but flush it away as soon as possible after it has done its work.

If you find an acid- or alkali-based cleaner is not doing the job, as a last resort try an abrasive cleaner like BAR KEEPERS FRIEND or T. L. SEA MARINE CLEANSER. On surfaces that are deeply stained, tarnished, or oxidized, the finely abrasive ingredients in these cleaners will abrade away the stain. They will do no harm if used sparingly, but repeated, aggressive use of abrasives on fiberglass will wear away the gelcoat.

# Maintenance: The Steps

There are three steps to good maintenance: clean, prepare, and protect. Almost every maintenance or restoration project should be approached in this three-step process. This is the key to success.

- ▶ First the surface is *cleaned*.

- ▶ Second, the surface is *prepared* by restoring its original characteristics. For example, this might mean polishing, removing oxidation, or sanding.

- ▶ Third, the surface is *protected* by a product that will isolate the surface from chemical or physical damage. Waxes, paints, varnishes, and other protective coatings provide the necessary surface protection.

Most hard surfaces on a modern recreational boat are fiberglass, plastic, wood, or metal. Generic care for these surfaces is a simple process of cleaning, preparation, and protection. While fiberglass, plastic, wood, and metal require slightly different techniques to maintain, the steps are the same. Depending on the severity of the problem, follow these steps. The chapters that follow will amplify this process for each of the major surface materials.

## Fiberglass

### MILDLY DIRTY (SEE CHAPTER 2)

- Clean by scrubbing with diluted boat soap and rinsing
- No further preparation is required
- Protect by waxing or polymer polishing the surface

### MODERATELY OXIDIZED

- Clean by scrubbing with diluted boat soap and rinsing
- Prepare by applying a moderate oxidation remover
- Protect by waxing or polymer polishing the surface

### SEVERELY OXIDIZED

- Clean by power-washing the surface
- Prepare by applying a heavy-duty rubbing compound to remove oxidation
- Protect by waxing, polymer polishing, or coating the surface

## Wood

### MILDLY SOILED VARNISH OR COATING (SEE CHAPTER 3)

- Clean to remove soil from the surface
- No further preparation is required
- Protect by wiping with chamois after boat wash down

### MODERATELY DEGRADED COATED FINISH

- Clean soil from surface
- Prepare with a light sanding
- Protect with a touch up coat of varnish or paint

### SEVERELY DEGRADED COATED SURFACE

- Clean with solvent and/or detergent
- Power sand to remove deteriorated varnish or paint
- Protect with appropriate number of coats of varnish or paint

## Metal

### MILDLY CORRODED (SEE CHAPTER 4)

▶ Clean with a detergent scrub

▶ No further preparation is required

▶ Protect with wax or polymer polish

### MODERATELY CORRODED

▶ Clean with a metal cleaner

▶ Prepare surface with metal polish

▶ Protect with wax or polymer polish

### SEVERELY CORRODED

▶ Clean by sandblasting or power-washing (keels and lower units)

▶ Prepare a smooth surface with bronze wool or wire brush

▶ Protect with wax, polymer polish, or a protective coating

# Essential Housekeeping

Constant vigilance prevents problems. The best route to a safe and beautiful boat is to use your eyes and hands constantly. Look at everything, even if you inspected just last week. Look again. Run your hands over the woodwork, under fuel filters, behind pumps. By getting up-close, you will feel the roughness in the varnish as degradation begins. A slow drip from the fuel filter will show up as a wet stain on your finger. Is there an odd smell coming from the engine compartment? Wiggling the hose at the water pump may disclose a loose clamp. By this simple touch-and-see technique you will often find a problem in its early stages.

## Protection from Weather

Cover whatever you can, to protect the boat from sun and salt. As the years pass, it will become evident that covered parts remain as good as new. When you remove a deck fitting, look underneath; the hidden fiberglass should look as new as it was the day the boat came out of the mold. Wax, or polymer polish, has an important role as a transparent layer that protects fiberglass, metal, coated wood, plastic, and glass—almost anything exposed to the elements.

## Clean, Clean, Clean

Clean and lubricate all moving parts as specified by the manufacturers. They usually know what's best for their products. There is nothing that preserves a boat better than cleanliness.

Dirt kept off the boat, or outside the cabin, is dirt that doesn't need to be cleaned. Place a welcome mat on the dock where you step aboard. The fiber varieties will deteriorate quickly but they offer a cheap way to keep dirt off the boat. A square of Astroturf will work as well. Put a bathroom rug at the foot of the companionway to catch all inbound dirt and sand. Take off your shoes when coming into the cabin.

Do everything you can to keep the boat dry and salt-free. Salt is a desiccant, meaning it absorbs and holds enormous amounts of water. Once a fabric is soaked with salt water, it will almost never completely dry because the salt continues to pick up water from the atmosphere. Try to store the sails dry and salt-free. Wait for a calm, clear day when you can run the sails up at the dock. Spray them with freshwater and let them dry in the sun. Racing sailors know that clean sails weigh considerably less than salt-encrusted canvas. Rinsing the sails lowers the overall weight of their boats and will probably improve performance. After an outing, rinse the deck with freshwater. Wipe the chrome and stainless steel with a chamois. Get rid of the salt.

Likewise, adequate ventilation is critical to creating a pleasant environment below deck. Get fresh air into closed areas as often as possible. Every few weeks, open all the lockers, floorboards, and lazarettes for an overnight airing. It will pay off in the long run by preventing bad smells, mold, and rot.

## Beat the Sun

To hold the temperature down on hot days, try covering ports and hatch covers with a tinted see-through film sold under the name SOLAR STAT. It comes in sizes large enough to cover a typical hatch or port. To apply it, you merely smooth it on with the supplied squeegee. Static electricity makes the plastic adhere, but it can be easily removed by peeling back a corner.

Or you can try the sunshades by OCEANAIR, which are attached to the headliner above a port to give added privacy and protection from the heat. The shades pull down like conventional window shades and a heat-reflective backing keeps the sun at bay. You can also attach them so they slide horizontally beneath a deck hatch. When not in use, the shades roll up inside a plastic enclosure.

## Maintenance Equals Safety

Regular maintenance will almost always reveal equipment failure before it's too late. By cleaning fiberglass often, you will put your hands on every inch of it, finding breaks and cracks as they develop. By polishing metal, you will discover loose screws, missing cotter pins, and the first signs of corrosion. Detect problems early and address them.

A piece of equipment that has been kept clean and maintained according to the manufacturer's directions will seldom fail. We put enormous trust in marine hardware and expect it to withstand tremendous punishment. We lean on lifelines. A single bow cleat separates us from disaster. A boat is made up of thousands of parts that must always work. Safety is no accident; it must be earned. Only equipment in good condition can be relied on to keep the crew safe.

# Cleaning Supplies

Here is a list of the most common cleaning materials you'll need. Always keep a good supply on your boat, so there's never an excuse to put a job off because you don't have the right equipment at hand.

### NYLON MESH

Nylon mesh is a nearly universal cleaning material, and yet it's a well-kept secret. It's inexpensive, it doesn't scratch, and it's easy to clean and reuse. Unfortunately, it's also very hard to find. Try the fabric department at Walmart for a nylon mesh made by MANDEL. It sells for under a dollar a running yard. If you can find it, nylon mesh with large net holes will not clog up with gunk as easily as the fabric grade does. Buy a few yards, and wad it up for almost any cleaning job.

### SYNTHETIC SCRUBBING PADS

There are surprisingly few good scrubbing pads on the market. Most clog with food, grime, or whatever you are cleaning. WILLIAMS SONOMA stores sell a colorful synthetic scrubbing pad, about the size of a cake of soap, that, unlike many others, does not clog with food particles. These pads are quite firm, which makes them easier to use on big jobs than nylon mesh. They don't scratch, are not impregnated with detergent, and seem to last forever. They are the best I have ever used.

Another good product is 3M SYNTHETIC STEEL WOOL. It's a combination of synthetic fibers and abrasive materials that performs like steel wool but doesn't rust, and is kinder to your fingers. This product can scratch surfaces, so proceed carefully.

### BRONZE WOOL

Bronze wool is rust-resistant and excellent for polishing metal, refurbishing teak, and general cleaning. Steel wool should never be used on a boat as it will shed tiny iron particles that will rust within days. These shards of metal always find a deep crevice to slip into and do their damage.

### DIAPERS

Baby diapers are excellent for cleaning up oil spills. They are the world's best "picker-uppers." Rather than spending money on expensive oil-absorbent cloths at the marine store, get some disposable diapers and place them, opened up, below the engine to catch stray drips. I've never had a boat without some on board.

### PSEUDO-CHAMOIS CLOTH

Sick of water spots? Automotive stores carry pseudo-chamois cloths that are excellent for drying varnished wood, chrome, and stainless steel to spot-free perfection. They work as well as a natural chamois but are tougher and won't disintegrate as easily as the real McCoy.

### PAPER TOWELS

There are endless uses for disposable paper towels. I go through a roll a week, and the boat isn't fouled by a lot of smelly rags.

### MOIST TOWELETTES

All new parents know about these moist, tough, yet soft tissues, which are marketed under many names and with many purposes. PAMPERS BABY

FRESH towelettes come in a convenient leak-proof plastic box and are ideal for many jobs—a throwaway rag to pick up spills quickly in the galley, a wet rag to wipe along interior corners to pick up dust, or a hand-cleaner when you can't leave the cockpit. The towelettes contain propylene glycol, aloe, and lanolin, which are quite benign ingredients.

## HAND CLEANERS

Grease will be much easier to remove from your hands if you rub them with VASELINE INTENSIVE CARE lotion or petroleum jelly before you begin a greasy job. Clean grease from your hands with baking soda and water. LAVA BAR SOAP also works well; the pumice it contains is abrasive and cleans off oil and grease. A marine product called LAN-LIN combines lanolin, pumice, and aloe to remove most petroleum-based stains effectively.

## RAGS AND CLOTH TOWELS

Collect old T-shirts and terry-cloth towels from home and keep them in your cleaning products locker. Most projects will require a clean rag for anything from cleaning and drying a surface to applying a compound. If you run out of old shirts, don't move into the main wardrobe: marine and hardware stores also sell bags of T-shirt material.

## SPONGES

Sponges are a source of disagreement. Natural sponges have their die-hard advocates who swear there is no substitute for the softness and absorbency of the sea's own product. Boaters who swear by synthetic sponges point out how natural sponges tear and don't come in the useful shapes of the synthetics. All agree that sponges are endlessly useful and no boat should be without them. I keep both types on board and decide based on the job at hand.

Before tossing out a smelly synthetic sponge, try heating it in a microwave oven for a minute or two. If the sponge is reasonably clean, the microwave oven will dry and sterilize it, giving it a second life. A natural sponge should be washed with soap and water and dried in the sun. Microwaving will destroy the composition of nature's product.

## BRUSHES

Bristle brushes of every size and description make cleaning easier. The ubiquitous dustpan and brush is quite effective on the boat. Hardware and marine stores offer brushes in varying widths, wide for sweeping big open spaces and narrow for tight spots. STAR BRITE sells a line of brushes with polypropylene bristles that come in differing stiffness—soft yellow bristles for gentle jobs, blue medium bristles for average cleaning, and stiff white bristles for serious scrubbing.

A toothbrush is sometimes the only tool that will scrub in small spaces. It is cheap and easily disposable. Since discovering how useful toothbrushes are, I never turn down my dentist's offer of a free one, although I must admit I've gotten some funny looks from my neighbors at the marina when they see me using a toothbrush around the edges of a deck cleat.

Some spaces you try to clean are so tight that you can't even move a toothbrush back and forth. Why not try using an electric toothbrush, equipped with a used brush and soaked in cleaner, to reach difficult places? Just place it on the dirty spot and let it vibrate the area clean.

A small bronze brush the size of a toothbrush is a perfect tool to remove rust, corrosion, and grime from tight areas. It will also do a great job of cleaning saws, drills, and other tools without scratching the metal. However, remember that once you have used anything to clean rust—a brush, a rag, or bronze wool—it will be contaminated by the rust. If not cleaned thoroughly, these cleaning materials may spread rust the next time they are used.

Get a copy of the FULLER BRUSH catalog. It has an unbelievable selection of specialized brushes for cleaning that would satisfy any boating application you can imagine.

### MIRRORS

A small unbreakable mirror allows you to see out-of-the-way places like the dark corners in back of the engine. Marine catalogs sell mirrors fixed on long staffs. Of course, with a two-foot stick, some duct tape, and a mirror, anyone can fashion a substitute.

### CARPET SWEEPERS

Remove or shorten the handle of a manual carpet sweeper to create a compact cleanup tool effective in the boat's tightest spaces. Using a sweeper with a full-length handle invites a bull-in-the-china-shop scenario.

### VACUUM CLEANER

A 12-volt wet-dry vacuum cleaner is inexpensive and does the job of two single-purpose machines.

## Clothing

Throughout the book, I will be recommending some products that call for special handling, such as cleaners containing strong alkalis and acids. It is advisable to wear protective clothing to guard against burns, toxic ingredients, and harmful fumes. Always read the cautions and safety instructions on the label before using a product. Do not assume that warnings have been put on the label only to shield the manufacturer from liability.

Before beginning any cleaning or coating project, take a moment to consider what contaminants you'll be working with. Will you produce toxic dust as you sand off bottom paint? When you apply contact cement to reattach the cabin headliner, will you expose yourself to hazardous fumes within the confines of the cabin? Will the acid in a commercial rust cleaner hurt your hands? These are basic questions to ask yourself before beginning a project involving dust or chemicals.

## Protective Clothing

Most of the time, you will only need to be concerned with protecting your eyes and hands.

### GLASSES AND GLOVES

To keep dust and debris out of your eyes, get a pair of 3M SAFETY GLASSES. They fit over prescription glasses and should always be worn when operating power tools and applying chemicals.

Many marine cleaners contain oxalic acid, phosphoric acid, or sodium hypochlorite. No matter how tough your hands may seem to be, you should wear protective gloves whenever working with cleaners, solvents, or unfamiliar chemicals. Regular work gloves are good for working around sharp, dirty, or rusty parts, but they can't protect your hands from solvents and cleaning chemicals. The acids and alkalis in strong cleaners can literally take the skin off your hands. Chemical-resistant gloves are available in hardware stores. Thin, disposable surgical gloves are excellent for working with messy products. When I'm using epoxy, I wear three or four surgical gloves on each hand and simply remove a layer when it gets too gunked up. Surgical gloves are easy to come by in marine stores and drugstores. PLAYTEX LIVING GLOVES are sturdier than surgical gloves, and they are lined, which makes them easier to pull on and off. To remove rubber gloves, first run them under cold water. They will pull off more easily when chilled.

### COVERALLS

For potentially hazardous projects, such as removing bottom paint or applying solvents, consider wearing TYVEK disposable coveralls. These hooded, roomy suits are cool and have elastic at the wrists and ankles. They can be had for about $10 and offer excellent protection. For spur-of-the-moment protection, try fashioning a trash-bag apron: cut arm and head holes in a trash bag to create a temporary coverall.

### MASKS AND RESPIRATORS

When it comes to breathing protection, you have a number of choices depending on the severity of the contaminant. Limited protection is afforded by paper dust-masks that cover the mouth and nose. These come in a variety of grades, do a fair job of filtering out airborne particles, and are adequate for most cleaning projects. Look for them at marine and hardware stores. At the other end of the spectrum are respirators such as the 3M SERIES 6000 and 7000 respirators to be worn when spray painting or using toxic solvents.

### EARPLUGS

Noise protection is not normally a concern, except when sanding. I've gotten by with pliable foam earplugs. Hard-toe shoes might be worth considering if you are working around heavy equipment.

## Cold-Weather Clothes

It's always colder on the water than it feels when you are at home. Put on many layers of clothes in preference to one heavy parka. Natives of cold climates know that multiple, lighter layers trap body heat and keep you warmer. The last layer should be a windbreaker.

Save retired long-sleeved shirts and long pants for the really dirty jobs like bottom painting. If you don't have a pair of foul-weather boots, use tennis shoes or sailing shoes, as they give good protection from slipping on a wet deck. The ribbing on the shoe soles wears off quite easily so keep an eye on how much tread is left.

Whenever you must kneel for a long time, wear kneepads. They can make all the difference in your comfort—and therefore, in your concentration.

# Cleaning Compounds

Many useful cleaners are probably already on the boat and are almost always found at home. Look in your medicine or kitchen cabinets for everyday remedies such as rubbing alcohol, dish soap, bleach, and ammonia. In the kitchen, you'll probably find white vinegar, baking soda, salt, tea, and lemons. As we shall see, these everyday natural products can often be used in place of brand-name cleaners. Don't overlook homebrew cleaners that have stood the test of time. Like the weather rhymes, home cures wouldn't continue to be used if they didn't actually work. Lemons aren't plastered with promises like marine products, but they often do the job just as well.

Try baking soda for cleaning any smooth surface. It is a mild, environmentally safe, yet effective cleaner that has been used by professionals for years.

## Marine Products

Even as you discover effective natural products and cheaper nonmarine cleaning compounds, don't forget that marine products are specifically designed to work in the harsh environment of salt, radical temperature change, and neglect. Most of these products are effective if you follow the manufacturer's directions. What normally separates one product from another is ease of application or longevity. If product A performs as well as product B, but goes on more easily, it will become more popular. If product C lasts longer than product D, it will be a favorite.

Most of us stick with a product if we feel it does an adequate job. Complacent, we rarely find out if there is something better out there. It is human nature that we hesitate to try new products. Brand advertising was invented to promote customer loyalty, and we seldom switch once we find a serviceable product. New and improved cleaners and polishes come into the market on a regular basis. Try some of the products recommended in this book that are unfamiliar to you. Chances are, you will find an improvement.

## The Fine Print

Printed on the back of every product is a long list of instructions and cautions, often in the smallest print possible. Our tendency is to ignore the instructions and plunge right into the project. As I've said, most products will do a decent job if they're used as intended. Manufacturers always test their products, and, in the process, determine how to obtain the best results. They want their products to succeed. Put on the reading glasses and pore over the fine print. It might make the job easier and will definitely make it more successful. Whenever you use commercial products, follow the label precautions exactly. For example, never mix cleaners containing ammonia and bleach. Harmful fumes can be created by the chemical reaction.

---

### Industrial Strength Cleaners

The first time I used CASTROL SUPER CLEAN at full strength, I simply thought of it as an excellent cleanser. It burrowed in and cleaned everything. Unfortunately, I hadn't read the label carefully or I would have noticed that sodium hydroxide (lye) is an ingredient. Two days later, layers of skin began coming off my fingers. Wear protective rubber gloves whenever you use powerful cleaners at full strength.

---

## Specialized Products

Single-purpose cleaning products, advertised to do just one specific task, are sweeping the market. Products were once billed as being capable of many cleaning jobs, but some companies are now expanding their lines by offering a whole slew of single-purpose cleaners to increase sales. Often there are only subtle differences between them; the intended result, apparently, is that buyers will fill their cabinets with half-used containers. This can be a problem if you postpone a chore because you don't have the exact product you were told would do the particular job you're tackling. Putting off a job may mean forgetting it. Why wait to get a specialized product when a more generic cleaner would do the job just as well? There's probably a product already on the boat that would suffice. For example, if there were no black streak cleaner in the locker, you'd probably have success removing the streaks with ordinary boat soap. *Boat Maintenance* will help solve this quandary by pointing out products such as WINDEX and BOAT ZOAP that cover a wide range of uses.

## Environmental Concerns

The environmental impact of adding chemicals to the waste stream is a large and complex subject beyond the scope of this book. However, it behooves us all to be aware of our relationship with the marine environment and to use chemical products responsibly. The careless use of cleaners can introduce harmful chemicals into our environment. Obviously we must exercise great caution with highly toxic products like acetone. Likewise, ingredients that are not toxic, but that are highly disruptive to the natural environment, must be used carefully. For example, most manufacturers of cleaning products have stopped using phosphates because their excessive nutrients can trigger algae blooms and die-offs, upsetting entire ecosystems. Whenever possible, we should consider using "green" or biodegradable products—cleaners that will break down biologically into harmless byproducts. Responsible manufacturers are bringing more green products to the market. As often as possible, I'll include suggestions on how to select and use products to minimize environmental impact.

Government regulations aimed at producing environmentally friendly products continue to multiply. Some states, such as California, have established laws calling for more rigid labeling and information than the Federal Government requires. Thanks to legislation (notably the Federal Clean Water Act) and public concern about the environment, major steps have been taken through the Environmental Protection Agency and corresponding state agencies to minimize the impact of chemicals being introduced into our waste stream. Marinas and ordinary gas stations have receptacles to collect waste oil and fuel. Batteries are returned to the manufacturer for disposal. The nozzles of gasoline pumps are fitted with rubber collars to capture fumes. Tributyltin, a highly toxic chemical, has been removed from bottom paints available to consumers. Many solvent-based paints are now manufactured with higher solid contents, which means that smaller amounts of toxic solvents evaporate as the paint dries. Manufacturers of cleaning products have consistently moved toward biodegradable ingredients. All of this is progress, but it's far from finished. Until the consumer refuses to purchase products disruptive to the environment, harmful chemicals will continue to be released into the waste stream.

We tend to assume that environmentally friendly products are less effective than their harsher counterparts—that using "green" products will always involve a tradeoff in effectiveness. This simply isn't true. For example, SIMPLE GREEN is a concentrated, powerful grease-buster that is nontoxic, noncorrosive, biodegradable, and contains no harsh chemicals. Even consumers for whom environmental impact is not the top priority should try the green products suggested here and elsewhere.

It's human nature to reach immediately for a product you know will clean anything. But why not try a gentler cleaner first? Being kind to your boat and the environment might mean taking a few extra minutes, but it's worth it. Start with the mildest cleaner and work up to the stronger stuff only if necessary. For example, begin cleaning dirty fiberglass with a gentle, environmentally safe cleaner like BOAT ZOAP. If this doesn't do the job, move to a medium-grade stain remover like FSR. If all else fails, pull out CASTROL SUPER CLEAN, your killer cleaner that can take the skin off an alligator. But save this as a last resort. You'll be surprised how often a gentle cleaner will do the job.

Generally, "home remedies" such as baking soda or lemons are nontoxic and environmentally the safest cleaners. They tend to be naturally milder, less expensive, and friendlier to your health. Consider these remedies instead of powerful, harsh cleaners that will do the job easily but might damage the surface permanently. If used incorrectly, super-cleaners can sometimes etch the surface, allowing dirt and corrosion to adhere more easily the next time. For example, if alkaline household cleaners like FANTASTIK are allowed to dry on fiberglass, they may eventually etch the surface. If you do use them, be certain to rinse them off before they have a chance to dry. Some environmentally sound ingredients used in commercial products also are far from innocuous. For example, lye can burn your skin, and ammonia will produce noxious fumes.

By choosing environmentally safe products, boaters will minimize their impact on the environment. It is currently impossible for consumers to determine the health and safety effects of every cleaning, painting, or maintenance product on the market just by reading labels. The U.S. government requires manufacturers to file Material Safety Data Sheets (MSDS) that identify the major hazardous ingredients in each product. But consumers will not normally see an MSDS sheet unless they request it from the manufacturer. (Occasionally, you will find a retailer who provides MSDS sheets.) All a consumer has to go by is the primary hazardous ingredient nearly always identified on the label. However, the ingredient listed may not be the only unsafe or environmentally harmful agent; it may not even be the *worst* offender. Current labeling regulations don't give us a foolproof system, but they're the only protection we have. The main active ingredients of all products mentioned in this book are listed in the Chemical Ingredients appendix. By checking appendix 4, you will find those products with active components that may be harmful to your health and to the environment. If you wish, you may avoid those you consider unsafe and choose a substitute.

# *Quick-Reference Guide*

## General Care

| TOPIC | JOB | PAGE | PRODUCT | HOW TO DO JOB |
|---|---|---|---|---|
| **Cleaning supplies** | Scrubbing | 12 | **MANDEL NYLON MESH** | Wad up a half-yard of nylon mesh and use as a scrubber. |
| | Scrubbing pads | 12 | **WILLIAMS SONOMA** scrubbing pads; **3M SYNTHETIC STEEL WOOL** | Use either product with detergent for general cleaning. |
| | Towelettes | 12 | **PAMPERS BABY FRESH** | Wet, tough, soft, disposable tissues with hundreds of uses. |
| **Clothing** | Using strong cleaners | 15 | **PLAYTEX LIVING GLOVES** | Wear protective gloves when using strong cleaners or solvents. |
| **Greasy hands** | Cleaning | 13 | **VASELINE INTENSIVE CARE** | Coating hands with lotion makes it easier to clean off grease. |
| | Removing grease | 13 | **LAVA BAR SOAP** | Pumice-containing soap helps abrade grease off. |
| **Cleaners** | "Green" cleaners | 17 | **CASTROL SUPER CLEAN** | Very powerful, environmentally safe cleaner for tough projects. |
| | | 18 | **SIMPLE GREEN** | Moderately strong cleaner with no harsh ingredients. |

# 2
# FIBERGLASS

**F**iberglass is the first hard surface we will consider. By fiberglass, I mean the entire structure of a modern fiberglass recreational boat: the hull, the deck, and structural members. This "shell" is composed of multiple layers of fiberglass fabric "frozen" in cured polyester resin. In a typical fiberglass boat, the hull, the deck, and the cabin structure are built in molds. First, a release agent such as silicone is applied to the surface of the mold so that the finished section can be removed cleanly. Then an initial layer of pigmented polyester resin is sprayed onto the mold; this first layer will be the gelcoat, the gleaming exterior surface we cherish. The hull or any other section is then built up with layers of fiberglass mat and roving saturated with resin. When the laminate has fully cured, the section can be removed from the mold.

Although they are advertised as maintenance-free, fiberglass boats are not without challenges. Boat manufacturers take great care to ensure that resin and hardener are mixed in the correct ratios, that proper curing times are observed, and that the fiberglass reinforcement is thoroughly wet out with resin. Nonetheless, problems can occur. As we shall see in chapter 5, a pocket of uncured resin may eventually absorb water and produce a gas within the laminate that will eventually cause blisters in the hull. Amines from the hardener will sometimes blush to the surface, causing the coating above to fail. Some residual silicone-release agent will always be present in the gelcoat and will need to be removed with solvent before any coating has a prayer of adhering to the fiberglass surface. As the outermost layer of the laminate, the gelcoat is continually exposed to weathering and abuse. Yet, for all these potential problems, fiberglass made the construction of modern pleasure boats economically feasible, and this book will concern itself with fiberglass boats. We will not attempt to cover the unique problems of wood, steel, aluminum, and ferroconcrete boats.

Here, we will address the problems that afflict fiberglass and how to prevent or cure them. We will look at the cleaning, preparation, and protection steps involved in routine care of fiberglass, as well as the treatment of more seriously neglected fiberglass.

Cleaning will always be the first step. If all you have to do is remove surface dirt, a conventional product like BOAT ZOAP will do an excellent job. If used as directed, it will not be so abrasive as to remove the polish or wax already protecting the surface. If there is moderate soiling, such as bird or spider droppings, scuff marks from street shoes, or waterline stains, a more robust cleaner will be required. Try FANTASTIK for spot cleaning and FSR for waterline scum. These cleaners will remove wax or polish, so the protective layer must be reapplied (see below). Finally, in the most severe case we will consider, if the gelcoat itself has dulled or become chalky, you will have to literally rub away the topmost layer of the compromised gelcoat with an oxidation remover before protecting it with a wax or polish.

# Oxidation

The question most frequently heard in the maintenance aisles of a marine store probably is: "What can I do about the dull look of my topsides?" One commonly sees older fiberglass hulls where the once-shiny surface has turned flat, or even chalky. The gelcoat is a combination of polyester resin, color pigments, and fillers, and is the frontline defense against the damaging effects of sunlight, salt water, drastic temperature change, dirt, and abrasion. When the exterior gelcoat surface begins to fail, oxidation is the form it takes. As the gelcoat ages, the surface resin literally wears away on a microscopic level. Eventually, enough resin will be destroyed by the elements that naked pigment particles will be exposed. You will initially notice this effect as a roughness and dullness in the once-gleaming surface. Waxing no longer brings back the original shine. Left to its own devices, mild oxidation will become severe. Severe oxidation has occurred when you pick up a chalky residue by running your hand across a white topside. You have literally wiped loose pigment particles off onto your hand.

But all is not lost. To postpone or even prevent oxidation, keep fiberglass surfaces clean and protected with a good coating of wax or polish. A new boat should have a protective wax or polish applied as soon as possible. (One exception occurs when topsides are painted with AWLGRIP or one of the other linear polyurethanes. See Linear Polyurethane sidebar, page 27.) If oxidation does occur, you need to apply an oxidation remover to rub off the loose, unbound particles, smooth out the microscopic pits, and expose the fresh, shiny gelcoat beneath. Once you have exposed smooth gelcoat, a good protective wax or polish will keep the surface shiny. A successful oxidation removal project will make the gelcoat look almost new.

Oxidation removers are formulated for mild, moderate, or severe cases of fiberglass oxidation. Mild oxidation has occurred when shiny fiberglass gelcoat begins to look slightly dull. Moderate oxidation is when the surface is completely dull and barely gives a reflection. Severe oxidation has occurred when a chalky substance can be wiped off the gelcoat with your hand. Most manufacturers offer an oxidation remover for each degree of severity. Don't be tempted to use a severe oxidation remover on a mild case. Oxidation removers are rubbing compounds and employ abrasives to do their work. If you use a remover designed for severe oxidation on a mild case, you will remove the oxidation all right, but you will also cut into and remove good gelcoat unnecessarily. The gelcoat is a thin layer. Abrade it as little as possible.

Two highly recommended oxidation removers are BOATLIFE LIQUID FIBERGLASS RUBBING COMPOUND AND COLOR RESTORER and 3M MARINE FIBERGLASS RESTORER AND WAX. The 3M product not only removes the oxidation but also leaves a wax on the fiberglass surface, although for better protection I would put more wax or polish over it. A nonmarine product, BAR KEEPERS FRIEND, if used carefully, can also do a good job of removing oxidation.

The secret of success with oxidation removers is to follow the label directions exactly. Most suggest that you apply the product and rub until the liquid disappears. Look at the cloth often. When you're removing oxidation from a boat with white topsides, the removed oxidation will come off the boat and onto the

rag as an ugly, gray, sticky mess. Change to a clean rag, or you will be wiping the removed oxidation back into the fiberglass, which can scratch the gelcoat. You want to buff the surface to a clean, high gloss.

## Wash Down after Every Cruise

You'll do far less cleaning and waxing if you wash down with freshwater after each trip out in the boat. It takes no more than 10 minutes to spray down the boat; for a few minutes more, you can wipe off the chrome and stainless steel with a chamois cloth. If your boat is out on a mooring, wash it down with a bucket of seawater and then rinse it with a small amount of precious freshwater. It's better than not washing down at all.

The chamois cloth prevents spotting of the bright metal and glass as the water dries, of course; but there are also other ways. My neighbor, who has a 47-foot Sea Ray, caught my attention by blow-drying his boat with a leaf blower. He said he'd been drying his cars for years with leaf blowers, and he figured it would work on his boat, too. Instead of spending half an hour cleaning up with a chamois, he gets the job done in only a few minutes, leaving his windshields and chrome rails perfectly spot-free.

## Fiberglass Restorers

After using an oxidation remover, some boaters follow with a fiberglass restorer such as NEW GLASS. Some oxidation removers, such as those suggested above, have the word "restorer" in their names, and should not be confused with these true restorers, which are actually coatings. Fiberglass restorers are acrylic polymers that create a protective coating over the gelcoat that will last longer than a wax. Although their formulations are proprietary, they behave like the acrylic floor polishes that give high gloss and dirt protection to vinyl floor tile.

If you wish to try a fiberglass restorer, you first need a clean, shiny surface without any trace of oxidation, but no additional preparation is required. Application normally is a tedious project involving many steps. With NEW GLASS, for example, you wipe on a first coat, wait a day, and then follow with four more coats. Be careful to mask off the waterline, the ports, and the rubrail so you can wipe the product right up to the edge. If it's not masked off, bottom paint, rubber, or trim paint can be streaked into the wet coating, which is difficult to remove. Its shiny, protective cover reportedly lasts for 12 to 24 months. When you need to redo NEW GLASS, you will first need to remove what's left of the old layer. Try using ARMSTRONG'S NEW BEGINNINGS EXTRA STRENGTH FLOOR CLEANER instead of the ammonia-based stripper the NEW GLASS manufacturer suggests. Spritz it on. Wipe it off, and rinse before applying a new coating of NEW GLASS.

## Waxes and Polishes

Once you have labored to expose a clean, shiny surface, you should apply a wax or polish immediately to preserve it. I use one or the other on almost every exterior surface of the boat. One exception to this rule concerns nonskid areas, where such a coating would make the deck too slippery for safety; keep nonskid surfaces clean by scrubbing frequently with boat soap. Incidentally, it's interesting to note that surfers use a wax to give their feet a grip on their boards, but it's a special and different wax, one that remains sticky, not slippery. Boat waxes and polishes buff up to a shiny, slippery surface that should be avoided on nonskid areas.

Years ago, all we had were conventional waxes, standard pastes made of carnauba and other natural waxes. Natural waxes crystallize and become glossy due to the heat of friction from a lot of hard rubbing. They're tedious to apply and last only a few months. In addition, they're soluble in petrochemicals such as gasoline, and have poor abrasion resistance. They are, however, proven performers. If you prefer a natural wax, I would suggest a marine carnauba wax such as COLLINITE'S #885 HEAVY DUTY PASTE FLEETWAX.

As synthetic polymer technology improved, manufacturers began to replace natural waxes with polishes having silicone polymers as the primary ingredient. The new synthetic polymers put a high-gloss layer on a clean gelcoat without the backbreaking work of polishing, and will last a whole season or more. Natural waxes like carnauba are now secondary components in many polishes, if they are used at all. The new polishes work well because the molecules link up in a web-like matrix without the heat of rubbing friction. As the solvent evaporates, reactive groups join together, creating this smooth matrix. If you look at a micrograph (a photograph produced by an electron microscope) of a new fiberglass surface, you will see microscopic pits even finer than those caused by oxidation. Wax molecules are too big to go into these holes and must bridge them. The new polymer polishes actually creep into these pits, seeking the lowest level, and build up until they form a slick, continuous surface. In a perfect world, all the crevices are filled, and soil and algae will find no purchase. No product is perfect, but synthetic polishes do a better job than natural waxes. An added advantage is that these new polymer polishes are more re-

## Missed a Spot?

Wear polarized sunglasses when you apply wax or polish. Any missed spots will stand out much better. You'll be able to see hazy, unbuffed areas; this is easier if you get your eyes close to the surface and look across it at a flat angle.

sistant to abrasion and solvents such as gasoline and acetone.

I have had excellent success with the newer polymer polishes such as STAR BRITE POLY SYSTEM ONE and STAR BRITE PREMIUM MARINE POLISH WITH TEFLON. 3M ULTRA PERFORMANCE PASTE WAX, a hybrid combination of waxes, fluoropolymer and silicone, is often singled out as a good performer.

# Deck

To clean the deck, wet the topsides first, so that dirty, soapy runoff won't streak the sides. Wet the deck, then scrub with BOAT ZOAP and a medium- or soft-bristled brush on a long handle. A narrow head on the brush allows easier access to tight spots. Look for a boat soap that is phosphate-free and biodegradable, such as BOAT ZOAP. Some people I interviewed asserted that floor-wax removers do a good job of removing stubborn stains. If you try one, remember to rinse thoroughly, as with any strong cleaner.

If there are stains that the boat soap failed to remove, try a fiberglass stain remover. Y-10 STAIN ABSORBENT GEL or FSR contain few or no abrasives, yet work well on tough stains. Rinse with freshwater after using. Rust spots on the deck call for special treatment. Apply MARYKATE SPRAY AWAY CLEANER to a rust spot, let it stand for a minute, and then rinse. This will frequently remove a rust stain from the deck. To remove rust spots from fiberglass decks, as well as to prevent rust from showing up on deck hardware, Caribbean charter operators favor RUST OFF (made by Boeshield). Dilute RUST OFF with water and apply it with a paintbrush to any rust spots on the fiberglass deck, to screws showing early signs of rust, and to any metal joint that is susceptible to rust. Rinse the entire deck thoroughly after allowing the compound to sit for about 30 minutes. The secret to using this product and similar rust cleaners is to give them time to work. It will remove rust from most nonporous surfaces. The product is nonflammable and biodegradable.

## Secrets of Professional Detailers

Professional boat detailers have their secret waxes and techniques, but they all share one vital truth: a good job can't be done with dirty rags. Clean rags are almost more important than the brand of wax or polish chosen. Use cheesecloth, terry cloth, or other soft rags, and change them often. When you see a dark, pencil-thin streak on the gelcoat, you are rubbing dirt back onto the boat. The rag has been used too long, and it's past time for a change.

A few professionals recommended the rectangular wax applicator pads obtained in automotive stores rather than the thinner round pads sold in marine supply stores. The thicker pads apparently hold their shape better after many washings.

## Up from the Deep

Bringing the anchor onto the foredeck can be a messy process if the bottom is mud. If you're like most of us, and don't have a hose connection up forward for cleaning, use a bucket of seawater brought up on a lanyard. Before bringing the anchor on board, I usually tie it off at the waterline and scrub it with a long-handled brush. It makes more sense to clean the anchor before you bring it on board. Even with the best arrangement, the deck around the anchor and chain will sometimes end up a mess after retrieval. Keep a spray bottle of diluted detergent and a terry-cloth towel in a net bag hanging in a clear area of the anchor locker. Use them for cleaning the muddy deck. If you have a pressurized saltwater system, you can run a hose from the galley saltwater spigot forward to the anchor locker to make cleaning up easier.

When you're looking for a quick project at the dock, pull your anchor, chain, and rode out of the locker and flake it out on the dock. Give it a good freshwater rinse and an airing. Ground tackle that is routinely stored wet and dirty will inevitably lose strength.

## Bird Droppings

Get to these stains as quickly as possible. Scrub with a soft-bristled brush and detergent. If a nonskid area is affected, just rinse; otherwise rewax the newly cleaned patch. If a purple stain remains, spot-clean with diluted bleach and rinse thoroughly before rewaxing the area. Avoid using strong bleach solutions as they may cause the fiberglass to yellow.

After a few rounds of scrubbing bird excrement, you may want to attack the problem more directly. Marine stores offer a range of bird deterrents, from inflatable snakes to the ubiquitous plastic owl. Eastern cruisers have had success keeping birds off the spreaders by hoisting a big wad of crumpled aluminum foil up the flag halyard. It reportedly works even better than the commercial products.

As a last resort, rub the most stubborn stains with bronze wool and Y-10. Rinse thoroughly to remove any cleaning residue and bronze-wool fibers.

## Topsides

Be gentle when you clean the topside gelcoat. It's tempting to scrub hard to remove stains and dirt, but remember, even with a mild boat soap, you are abrading a very thin gelcoat every time you scrub. Take it easy. If you aren't getting anywhere, try adding a little lemon juice.

As with the deck, you should determine whether the cleaner you have selected will remove wax or polish, as the stronger cleaners will. Try BOAT ZOAP first; it will not remove the polish. If that doesn't work, use a stronger cleaner like Y-10 or FSR, which will require you to apply a layer of polish to replace the one that was removed. As a last resort, carefully apply an oxidation remover or rubbing compound. Begin with a product formulated for mild oxidation. The area treated will have to be rewaxed after a thorough rinsing.

Black streaks on the topsides are a common complaint. I tried almost every cleaner on the market, looking for one that would take off the streaks but not remove the wax or polish. By accident, I discovered that BOAT ZOAP does just that when wiped on wetted topsides.

Cleaning and waxing the topsides is naturally much easier when the boat is berthed in a slip. Try adjusting the docking lines so that the section of the boat you are working on is brought closer to the dock. You will avoid a lot of stretching and muscle pain. If you're moored out, or at anchor, try cleaning the topsides from the dinghy. Stand in the dinghy and hold the boat with one hand. Put a long-handled brush through the inboard oarlock and brush the topsides clean with a back-and-forth motion with the other hand. Move carefully, and take care not to upset the dinghy when standing.

## Graphics, Letters, and Stripes

### Removing Painted Letters

Anyone who has changed states or bought a secondhand boat has probably had to contend with old lettering. If the paint has been in place for any length of time, the gelcoat underneath will have been protected from the elements and will not have oxidized, while the surrounding gelcoat will have aged normally. Once the paint is removed, the outline of the old letters will be obvious. The judicious use of a rubbing compound like **3M Super Duty Rubbing Compound** will blend these differing surface levels as well as remove any paint stain that has bitten into the gelcoat pores. It is a very abrasive compound, so proceed carefully; if you apply much pressure, you risk removing too much. Acetone is not a good choice for this job. Acetone is commonly thought to be such a good solvent that it can be used to remove anything, including paint. In fact, it takes an inordinate amount of effort to make it work, and acetone can harm the gelcoat if not removed immediately.

I've found that oven cleaner makes removing painted letters easier. Try removing painted letters using **Easy Off** oven cleaner. Immediately wipe up any oven cleaner that runs down where you don't want it. Leave it on for 10 to 20 minutes. The bubbled paint will peel off like a charm when scraped with a putty knife or a piece of nylon mesh. Wear rubber gloves when working with oven cleaners as they often contain lye or equally caustic chemicals. (Despite the warnings on the can not to use **Easy Off** on various surfaces, most of the people I interviewed agreed it does a good job.) You may find that painted letters have penetrated into the gelcoat. Again, a rubbing compound like **3M Super Duty Rubbing Compound**, applied carefully, will finish the job.

## Linear Polyurethane Finishes

Skillfully applied, a two-part linear polyurethane paint (LPU) will deliver extraordinary gloss and is the closest thing to a maintenance-free coating currently on the market. **Awlgrip** and **Interlux** both offer these paints. The mirror-like finish can be maintained by following a few simple rules suggested by **Awlgrip**'s manufacturer. (For more on these paints, see chapter 5.)

- Wash the LPU surface regularly with water and a mild detergent. Rinse well.
- Wipe the surface with a soft towel.
- Use white vinegar and hot water to remove salt stains.
- Clean off diesel soot stains from the stern with a mild polish such as **Y-10**.
- Do not wax LPU. Use wax only as a protective measure on small scrapes and scratches.
- Do not use abrasives to clean, as they will scratch the surface.
- Keep caustic or acid teak cleaners away from the topsides.
- Be careful of abrasion when covering the boat for winter. Use a canvas tarp and secure it well to avoid months of flapping. Leave some ventilation. Do not shrinkwrap.

If you are removing lettering from a newer boat, try **Meguiar's Mirror Glaze #49 Heavy Duty Oxidation Remover** to remove the remaining traces of paint without taking off gelcoat. Wipe the surface clean with mineral spirits before waxing or applying new lettering.

**Interlux** produces a paint remover named **Pintoff 299E**, designed to remove old paint from fiberglass, which, after application and removal, leaves a fairly clean surface. It doesn't contain the environmentally toxic and poisonous chemical methylene chloride and it won't burn your hands.

**2**

Quick-Reference Guide

## Quick-Reference Guide

### Fiberglass

| TOPIC | JOB | PAGE | PRODUCT | HOW TO DO JOB |
|---|---|---|---|---|
| **Cleaning** | Mild | 22 | BOAT ZOAP | Wet boat. Scrub with diluted detergent. Rinse. |
| | Spot-cleaning | 22 | FANTASTIK | Wet spot. Spray on FANTASTIK. Rinse. Rewax if not nonskid. |
| | Waterline stain | 22 | FSR | Wet topsides. Apply cleaner. Rinse. |
| | Oxidation | 23 | BOATLIFE LIQUID FIBERGLASS RUBBING COMPOUND AND COLOR RESTORER; 3M MARINE FIBERGLASS RESTORER AND WAX | Apply in small area, wiping with clean cloths until liquid is gone. Buff when compound is dry. Rewax. |
| | | 23 | BAR KEEPERS FRIEND | Scrub as above. Rinse. Apply wax or polymer, polish. |
| | Restoration | 23 | NEW GLASS | Wipe on. Wait a day. Apply 4 more coats as directed. |
| | Wax | 24 | COLLINITE'S #885 HEAVY DUTY PASTE FLEETWAX | Apply COLLINITE'S FLEETWAX to clean a surface. |
| | Polish | 25 | STAR BRITE POLY SYSTEM ONE; STAr BRITE PREMIUM MARINE POLISH WITH TEFLON; 3M ULTRA PERFORMANCE PASTE WAX | After applying oxidation remover and wiping off any residue, apply polymer polish. |

## Removing Graphics and Striping Tape

Old vinyl lettering and striping tape can be removed with the careful use of a heat gun or hair dryer, and a putty knife or scraper. Once the tape is off, use a paint remover, solvent, or a product called GOO GONE to clean up the adhesive residue.

A new product called STRIPE ELIMINATOR also does an outstanding job of removing striping without the use of heat guns or acetone. STRIPE ELIMINATOR is a small, round disk made of an eraser-like material. When attached to a variable-speed drill and run at low speed, it removes vinyl letters or stripes in seconds.

| TOPIC | JOB | PAGE | PRODUCT | HOW TO DO JOB |
|---|---|---|---|---|
| **Deck** | Dirty | 25 | **BOAT ZOAP** | Scrub with a soft brush and rinse. |
| | Heavy dirt | 25 | **Y-10 STAIN ABSORBENT GEL; FSR** | Wet deck. Apply to stain. Rinse. |
| | Rust spots | 25 | **MARYKATE SPRAY AWAY CLEANER** | Leave spray on spot for a minute. Rinse. |
| | Prevent rust | 25 | **RUST OFF** | Dilute with water. Brush solution on surfaces. Rinse after 30 minutes. |
| | Stubborn stains | 26 | **Y-10 STAIN ABSORBENT GEL**; Bronze wool | Wet area. Rub using bronze wool with **Y-10**. Rinse. |
| | Bird droppings | 26 | Bleach | Scrub with detergent. Spot with bleach. Rinse. Rewax. |
| **Topsides** | Dirty | 26 | **BOAT ZOAP** | Scrub with soft brush and freshwater. |
| | Stained | 26 | **Y-10 STAIN ABSORBENT GEL; FSR** | Wet topsides. Apply cleaner. Rinse. Rewax. |
| | Black Streaks | 26 | **BOAT ZOAP** | Wet area. Scrub with **BOAT ZOAP**. Rinse. |
| | Removing painted letter residue | 27 | **3M SUPER DUTY RUBBING COMPOUND** | Apply rubbing compound to paint stain remaining in gelcoat. Clean before new painting or graphics. |
| | Removing painted letters | 27 | **EASY OFF** oven cleaner | Spray on letters. Wipe up excess. 15 minutes later, scrape off with putty knife. Clean area. |
| | Removing painted letters | 27 | **INTERLUX PINTOFF 299E** | Environmentally safe paint remover. Apply. Scrape off paint. Clean. |
| | Remove graphics | 28 | **GOO GONE; STRIPE ELIMINATOR** | Carefully heat graphic tape with heat gun. Clean up residual adhesive with **GOO GONE**. Try rubber eraser disk called **STRIPE ELIMINATOR**. |

# 3 WOOD

In the marine environment, wood care often amounts to wood coating—the application of paint, varnish, or some other protective layer. Most untreated wood will not stand up to weathering. Sun, salt, moisture, and temperature variation will attack the wood fibers, causing swelling, rot, delamination, and warping. Protection is obtained by sealing off the wood from the effects of weathering. Much of the wood on recreational boats will be treated with paint, varnish, or some other protective coating. As a result, a lot of information on wood care is found in chapter 5, the chapter on coatings. The primary exception is untreated teak.

Paint or varnish must form a continuous membrane to offer effective protection from the elements. Nicks, scrapes, and gouges will open any coating and let moisture into the substrate. There's not much you can do about sun, moisture, and temperature changes except to keep the finish in sound condition. Don't wait until you see the finish deteriorate before applying touch-ups.

As with the gelcoat and most other surfaces on the boat, the best long-term protection for coated wood is a good coat of wax or polish. Wax or polymer polishes (see chapter 2) will do a great deal to protect any non-porous surface from the elements.

Teak is the most common wood used on boats, but by no means the only one. Mahogany and oak share many of teak's qualities and will probably be used more frequently for exterior trim on production boats as good-quality teak becomes increasingly rare and expensive. For interior uses, the builder has much greater latitude in selecting wood because weather resistance is not a factor.

# Boat Care on the Lakes

**David Brown** has written two boating books and submits a newspaper column on Great Lakes boating. Years ago, he was a charter-boat operator, and now he teaches U.S. Coast Guard Licensing courses. It is hard to pin him down on his preference for power or sail, as he has one of each kind of boat. But not so with the maintenance jobs he likes best. His true love is working with wood.

I was most interested in his comments on what makes boating on the Great Lakes different from using and maintaining pleasure craft on the sea coasts.

"The Lakes are different. Because our season is short and our water fresh, not salty, we have somewhat different needs. We get a lot of slime and grass on our bottoms, not the barnacles or mussels you get in salt water. If it weren't for the slime, we probably wouldn't need toxic bottom paint at all.

"Since we do our boating close to many big cities, environmental dirt is our biggest cosmetic problem, and because of it the most frequent headache is getting stains off the gelcoat. Lots of our boaters use **SOFT SCRUB** to clean the fiberglass surfaces and **ZUD** to scrub the teak. If we don't keep after teak it turns almost black, not a nice gray like you find in saltwater areas. **SIKKENS CETOL** is the most popular teak coating on the lakes.

"Now, with the advent of storing our boats for the winter under shrinkwrap, mildew has become a big problem if the cover is not vented properly.

"But because our bottoms don't need a lot of care and our decks are fairly easy to clean, Lake boaters tend to be more neglectful, since deterioration on their boats is slower. They often avoid keeping up with preventive maintenance. Seeing a problem is often the impetus a person needs to fix it. Lake boaters aren't constantly looking for problems and, unfortunately, can become negligent."

# Exterior Teak

Exposure to the weather breaks down the cellulose fibers in teak, causing it to turn a light gray. This is perfectly acceptable if you have no objection to gray wood. I've found that the best way to care for untreated teak is to rinse it with potable water after every outing. However, some boaters report that a saltwater washdown of, for example, a teak deck keeps the teak free of mildew and creates a nice, natural gray.

However, if you want to preserve the warm, golden color of freshly cut teak, your options are a protective coating or an oil treatment, applied in either case after a thorough cleaning. A full discussion of the various teak oils and coatings can be found in chapter 5. Here, I'll discuss the cleaning of the wood.

Teak cleaners differ from conventional wood cleaners in that they contain strong acids or alkalis to penetrate worn and weathered wood. These chemicals are strong enough to lift any varnish that is close by. They will cut into the anodized finish on aluminum, etch chrome, and damage gelcoat. Use these products with care. Always be prepared to flush the sur-

## Teak Bungs

Exterior teak is normally secured with deep-seated screws that are countersunk into the wood—when the screw is fully sunk, the head stops in a shallow recess lower than the surrounding surface. Small wooden plugs called "bungs" are then glued into the hole to hide the screw heads. These bungs have the unwelcome habit of coming off or breaking.

To remove an old teak bung, drill a pilot hole in the bung. Insert a screw and drive it down until it hits the screw below. Continue to turn the screwdriver until the bung breaks loose and backs out.

To replace a missing bung, first scrape out all of the old residue from the hole. Sand the bottom of the new bung to almost the depth of the bung hole, but leave at least a quarter inch protruding above the surface. Using **Q-TIPS**, wipe both the bung and the hole with acetone to remove residual oils. Put epoxy on the sides of the plug and the sides of the hole. Insert the plug with the grain aligned with the grain of the wood. When the adhesive has cured, carefully place the beveled side of a chisel on the protruding teak surface just behind the raised part of the new bung. Tap the chisel with a hammer. The excess will shear off cleanly. If necessary, carefully sand the top of the bung smooth, using 120-grit paper. Spot-treat the bung with varnish, oil, or whatever you use on your teak so that it matches the surrounding wood.

rounding area with potable water in case of spill or spatter. Use safety glasses and rubber gloves to protect yourself from splatters.

For a basic cleaning of untreated teak, use a good boat soap and scrub *across* the grain with a soft brush. Scrubbing *with* the grain gouges out the soft wood fibers. Put dry talcum powder on the teak to soak up any grease spots.

When boat soap isn't enough, BoatLIFE Teak Brite Teak Cleaner and Star brite Sea Safe Teak Cleaner are both environmentally sound marine products that do a good job of lifting the dirt out of teak. Both manufacturers offer an optional companion product, BoatLIFE Teak Brite Teak Brightener or Star brite Sea Safe Teak Brightener, to bleach the cleaned wood to a lighter shade, remove any residue from the cleaning step, and bring out the luster of your teak. These two steps should precede any coating or oiling of teak discussed in chapter 5.

To clean more seriously degraded teak, scrub the wood with Bar Keepers Friend, a nonmarine product that contains oxalic acid. Use lots of water when scrubbing and when cleaning up.

There are two-step cleaners on the market that I hesitate to mention because they begin with a highly alkaline agent that must be followed immediately with an acid rinse to neutralize the alkalinity. Applying just the right amount of acid to neutralize the alkaline is tricky, so you may be flushing a considerable amount of waste overboard that is strongly acid or alkaline. This caustic-acid combination can also remove a considerable amount of the soft teak grain, leaving ridges of hard grain. If you're not sure what kind of cleaner you're looking at, check the directions. Avoid two-step systems that call for the immediate application of the second component. The more environmentally friendly teak-cleaning systems mentioned above will allow ample time between the cleaning and brightening steps, and will not require immediate application of the second step.

Finally, as an alternative to the commercial products, the home-brew of choice for weathered teak is a 3-to-1 solution of liquid detergent and CLOROX plus a small amount of WEST MARINE TSP (trisodium phosphate). Scrub across the grain, but not so hard as to cut into the soft wood-grain lines. After five minutes, rinse thoroughly with potable water. You can now proceed to whatever finish you prefer. Don't sand teak unless absolutely necessary, as sanding removes too much soft wood and often pulls out loose teak bungs.

# Interior Wood

## Varnished Wood

On a production boat, all interior woodwork will probably be painted or varnished. Teak and holly are commonly used. Uncoated interior wood should be treated like fine furniture and protected with a furniture polish like PLEDGE. My own preference is to varnish wood below decks. It seals the wood with a durable, smooth finish that doesn't attract dust, and it allows a high-gloss, satin, or rubbed-effect finish, depending on your choice of varnish. Similarly, paint below deck will probably be high-gloss but can be satin or flat, depending on personal preference. Varnished interior flooring may be cleaned with MURPHY's OIL SOAP, another one of those great products that needs no rinsing.

Likewise, clean your varnished interior paneling much as you would the paneling in the den. FANTASTIK and spray-formula MURPHY's OIL SOAP are well accepted commercial wood cleaners that, used frequently, will keep cooking or heating grime from dulling interior wood finishes. Professional cleaners sometimes use an inexpensive 50/50 combination of white vinegar and lemon juice to clean generic gunk from wood surfaces. For a quick housecleaning, simply wipe the wood with a damp chamois.

Interior teak panels are typically teak-veneered plywood. The veneer is very thin and cannot be abraded too much or it will wear through. Use a mild detergent to clean the veneer surface.

## Painted Wood

For routine cleaning of painted wood surfaces I use MURPHY's OIL SOAP. For some reason, painted interior surfaces seem to attract mildew. I've found that white vinegar works well on mildew: wipe it on and then rinse it off with potable water. If you want heavier artillery, a mixture of CLOROX and turpentine will remove mildew and leave a light turpentine film on the painted surface to prevent mildew from forming again. The best way to prevent mildew is to promote the free movement of air throughout the boat.

## Untreated Interior Wood

The only *known* bare wood on the boat might be the cockpit teak, but sometimes untreated wood can be found out of plain sight—the back side of a varnished wood panel, or a backing block supporting a deck fixture. I would suggest you coat all such exposed surfaces to preserve them—or at least attempt to clean them occasionally to prevent mildew and rot. (Carpenter bees are also always looking for untreated wood in which to bore their holes.)

As we've seen, interior wood on a boat is normally treated in some way. If it hasn't been painted or varnished, it should at least be rubbed with furniture oil or treated with a furniture polish such as PLEDGE wax. Lemon oil, in particular, will keep mildew at bay as long as it remains on the surface of wood.

## Removing Dents

To repair a shallow dent in wood, place a wet towel over the spot and apply a hot iron. The moist heat will swell the wood and remove most of the indentation. (It may also raise varnish or paint, and necessitate a touch-up.) In the case of a deeper dent, poke a number of holes in the wood with a fine pin or needle. Steam from an iron will drive the heat down deep and should improve the overall results.

*Quick-Reference Guide*

# Wood

| TOPIC | JOB | PAGE | PRODUCT | HOW TO DO JOB |
|---|---|---|---|---|
| **Exterior teak** | Cleaning | 33 | BOAT ZOAP | Scrub across grain. Rinse. |
| **Deck teak** | Cleaning | 33 | BOATLIFE TEAK BRITE TEAK CLEANER; STAR BRITE SEA SAFE TEAK CLEANER; BAR KEEPERS FRIEND | Scrub across grain. Rinse thoroughly. |
| | Brightening | 33 | BOATLIFE TEAK BRITE TEAK BRIGHTENER; STAR BRITE TEAK BRIGHTENER | Apply after cleaning. |
| | Cleaning with home-brew | 34 | CLOROX; WEST MARINE TSP | Scrub across grain. Rinse thoroughly. |
| **Teak bung** | Removing | 33 | | Drill pilot hole in bung. Insert screw. Turn until bung comes out. |
| | Replacing | 33 | Q-TIPS; CETOL | Clean scraped-out hole with acetone. Epoxy the sides and bottom of bung. Shear off excess. Spot treat. |
| **Interior** | Cleaning | 34 | FANTASTIK; MURPHY'S OIL SOAP | Spray on. Wipe with clean cloth. |
| | Waxing | 34 | PLEDGE | Spray on. Wipe with clean cloth. |
| | Cooking grime | 34 | White vinegar; Lemon juice; MURPHY'S OIL SOAP; FANTASTIK | Clean with 50/50 vinegar and lemon juice. Or clean with FANTASTIK or MURPHY'S OIL SOAP. |
| **Painted surfaces** | Cleaning | 34 | MURPHY'S OIL SOAP | Spray on. Wipe with clean cloth. |
| | Mildewed | 34 | White vinegar | Wipe on. Wipe off with damp cloth. |
| | Prevent mildew | 35 | CLOROX; turpentine | Wipe a CLOROX-turpentine mix onto painted surface. Do not rinse. |
| **Wood dents** | Removing | 35 | Steam iron | Drill small holes. Apply steam. |

# 4 METAL

Your boat depends on myriad metal parts—fasteners, structural members, pumps, anchors, winches, and sinks. Each part requires constant care, or so it seems to the boatowner. To add to the complexity, a number of different metals are used and each has its own problems. How can a boatowner be expected to know how marine metals differ and interact? Why was each metal chosen for its job? How do you care for each metal and keep it functioning at 100 percent of its designed strength? The answers to these questions should begin with a better understanding of the metals themselves.

## Marine Metals

On a typical fiberglass sailboat, the mast and boom are made of aluminum because of the metal's light weight and excellent corrosion resistance.

Stainless steel is usually chosen for parts requiring high strength, as well as excellent corrosion resistance and machinability. Stainless parts are usually small but are located everywhere.

Bronze, often used for seacocks, is very strong and corrosion-resistant, and can be cast into highly refined shapes.

Brass is largely decorative, used in clocks and barometers.

Iron or lead keels, due to their enormous weight, are significant metal components of a boat but are only visible at haulout time.

In this chapter I discuss these metals one at a time, looking at why they were chosen by the designers and what can be done to maintain each.

What can go wrong with metal? Corrosion is the most common problem. On a boat, there are many sources of corrosion, some more obvious than others. The easiest of these to spot is weather-related deterioration or environmental damage. Black spots, streaks, and pitting can usually be traced to the environment. Acid rain is a major offender.

Then there is the boater's nemesis, electrolysis, or galvanic action, where electrical current flowing from one metal to an adjoining metal weak-

## Tools on Board

Metal tools designed for the home will not fare well in the high-humidity environment of a boat. The best defense against corrosion is to wipe petroleum jelly or **WD-40** on tools. Store metal parts and tools in plastic boxes or heavy canvas tote bags. Almost all metal storage containers will rust—and most are too bulky to fit in a locker anyway. Home Depot carries a line of canvas tool bags with dozens of pockets. Because the bags are soft, they fit into the tight, unusually shaped spaces common on a boat. Hardware stores also sell oil-impregnated papers that are used to line drawers and containers, and so delay the corrosion of tools. Ultimately, the best solution may be to leave your favorite tools on shore.

ens it to the point of destruction. This subject is covered in great detail by other authors and will only be touched on here (see sidebar on page 40). You should train yourself to look for the telltale signs of galvanic corrosion: mild "pinking" and pitting. If it's detected soon enough, any metal can be protected.

Rust is a particularly aggressive form of corrosion that afflicts ferrous metals (metals containing iron) in the presence of oxygen and water. Many metals react with oxygen and form a surface layer of oxidation. In the case of stainless steel, for example, this layer of oxidation is nonporous and adheres well to the substrate. This "corrosion" is, in effect, a protective coating. Stainless corrodes when this oxide layer is breached by microscopic impurities, scratches, or cracks in the surface. By contrast, on nonstainless ferrous metals, iron oxide (rust) forms. It is porous and does not adhere to the underlying metal. The oxide layer is neither protective nor stable. Once rust has begun, it will spread like a cancer, growing and shedding layer after layer as it encounters fresh iron to convert. Only protective coatings and polishes will keep rust from getting started on ferrous metals.

Problems relating to mechanical stress are more difficult to detect. Often the use of special dyes and a jeweler's loupe are required to reveal microscopic stress cracks unnoticeable to the naked eye.

Finally, metals age like everything else. Old metal, even if kept in excellent condition, will probably have lost much of its strength through years of stress and exposure.

What do you do when you suspect metal corrosion or failure has begun? Usually, the first sign that something is afoot is when the metal appears dirty, when it loses its luster. At this point, it is noticeable and correctable. Quick action with the proper cleaner, followed by a wax or polish, will stop surface deterioration. It may seem strange at first, but get into the habit of applying a wax or polymer polish to metal parts after you clean them. The metal will keep its finish much better than it will if you only clean it. (For more on waxes and polishes, see chapter 2.) Ferrous metals, including stainless steel, will often give a hint that something is starting to go wrong when a slight pink, rusty tint forms on screw threads or at a weld.

In increasing order of severity, the metal problems we will address are tarnishing, pitting, corrosion, and rust. Each has its cure. However, if you keep a clean boat, most of the more severe corrosion problems will never have a chance to get started.

# Aluminum

Contrary to popular opinion, aluminum is not a single product, but a generic term for a large category of alloyed metals created for different purposes. Aluminum alloys are lightweight compared to steel and bronze. Their alloys can be fabricated into complex shapes by all common metal-forming processes.

Aluminum alloys resist corrosion, readily accept a wide range of surface finishes, and are highly resistant to both heat and light. Aluminum's strength is greatly increased by adding small amounts of alloying elements or by heat treatments. A combination of alloying and heat-treating can produce an aluminum product that, pound for pound, is stronger than structural steel. Copper, magnesium, zinc, and silicon are the alloys used to impart differing characteristics to wrought (machined) aluminum. Cast aluminum, as you might imagine, is cast into a mold and not machined.

---

## Don't Try to Guess

Guessing at the size of a screw, or the gauge of an old wire, or the diameter of a hose needing replacement, is a hit-or-miss process at best. Remove the failed part, take it with you to a hardware or marine store, and get the correct size on the first trip.

Guessing almost always leads to frustrating returns and wasted effort. Time is better spent on the boat than on running back and forth.

---

## *Anodizing*

On boats, you will most often find aluminum parts are anodized. Anodizing aluminum is a process that creates a protective layer of aluminum oxide on the surface to a thickness of about 0.015 mm. (There is another method of treatment, called hard coating, that will increase the thickness of this protective aluminum oxide layer by 10 times.) Anodizing gives the aluminum part superior abrasion and corrosion resistance. Masts, booms, and aluminum deck fittings are therefore normally anodized. New masts and booms are, however, being painted with linear polyurethane finishes in preference to anodizing, a process increasingly looked on with disfavor by the Environmental Protection Agency as causing unacceptable pollution.

Whenever bare aluminum is exposed to the atmosphere, a thin transparent oxide skin forms immediately, which protects the metal from further oxidation. It is this self-protection that gives aluminum its high resistance to corrosion. If it is removed by cleaning or damaged by scratching, the oxide will form again.

Alkalis are among the few substances that attack the protective oxide skin and are therefore corrosive to aluminum. For this reason, cleaning agents containing alkalis should be avoided and only used if you want to remove the oxide skin.

Long-term aluminum corrosion will result from direct chemical attack, such as acid rain in an industrial area, or from electrochemical action—the dreaded galvanic action that most boaters are aware of.

# Galvanic Corrosion

Galvanic corrosion occurs when dissimilar metals are brought in contact in the presence of an electrically conductive fluid—for our purposes, salt water. A current begins to flow through the connection from the metal with the lower electrical potential (the "least noble" metal) toward the metal with the higher potential (the "most noble" metal). The reaction leads to the pitting, erosion, fatigue, and eventual failure of whichever metal happens to be the "least noble" in the pairing. The first signs of galvanic corrosion are mild pinking and pitting.

The metals commonly used on boats can be arranged in a hierarchy of electrical potential, up from the least noble metal used in boats, zinc. Taking the metals we consider, a basic ladder would look like this:

- zinc (least noble)
- aluminum alloys
- chrome
- cast iron
- brass
- copper
- bronze
- 304 stainless steel
- 316 stainless steel (most noble)

The greater the separation between metals on this ladder, the faster the corrosion will progress. This explains, for example, the poor performance of stainless-steel fasteners in aluminum spars. The difference in electric potential between the two metals is wide, and the electron flow from the aluminum to the stainless-steel screw will degrade the aluminum surrounding the screw; ultimately, the screw may seize up in the aluminum oxide created.

There are two basic approaches to preventing galvanic corrosion. The first is to separate or insulate dissimilar metals, thus breaking the direct electrical connection. In the case of a stainless fastener in an aluminum mast, insulation tape or bedding compound should be used on the screw threads to isolate one metal from the other.

The other approach, used when metal parts are immersed in sea water, is to add another metal to the mix, one that has no structural role and a lower electrical potential. Zinc has an electrical potential lower than any other metal commonly seen on boats, so it has assumed the role of a "sacrificial" metal. If sacrificial zincs are attached to metals you wish to protect, you can be sure that any stray current will flow from the zinc and destroy it, rather than the working part.

Sacrificial zinc anodes can be placed on propeller shafts, inside the engine, on hulls, or attached to outboard engines or stern drives—in almost any place where the potential for metal corrosion is anticipated. Commonly called zincs, these anodes should be replaced when they erode to about half their original size. If they need replacing more than once a year it may indicate an electrical discharge from a neighbor at your dock that will require prompt attention.

While your boat is in dock, you can fasten a large zinc to a heavy wire and immerse the zinc in seawater over the side. The inboard end of the wire should be attached to the boat's grounding system. Routine inspection of the zinc will alert you to any electric current coming from a boat docked close by. Stray electric current could well be affecting your boat's metal parts.

## Aluminum Care

First, decide if the corrosion on your aluminum should remain or be taken off. If the corrosion is mild, it is probably better to leave the protective surface oxides on the part. Surface dirt should be removed with a mild cleaner such as BOAT ZOAP.

However, if these oxides have become so severe that they wipe off like chalk, don't try to scrub them away with just any cleaner. Use a specialized marine product such as 3M ONE STEP ALUMINUM RESTORER AND POLISH (which is abrasive), or WEST MARINE METAL POLISH (which is petroleum-based), to clean the surface. A protective oxide layer will form again very soon.

> ## Photographing the Masthead
>
> Few of us spend enough time inspecting the upper reaches of the mast except when it is brought down for winter. The next time you go up the mast, take a camera. You can hold the camera over your head and take a number of shots of the masthead. You'll gain a much better sense of the setup in this rarefied region. The photograph might even show problems in the making that might not otherwise be known until the mast comes down at haulout time.

### ALUMINUM MASTS

Clean an aluminum mast with detergent and water when it is unstepped for the winter. Use bronze wool on the worst stains. The protective oxide will form again quickly, so in my experience there is no need to wax these surfaces. Now is also the time to clean and lubricate the halyard sheaves with a penetrating oil.

As we've seen, the combination of aluminum spars and stainless-steel fasteners is common, due to the great strength of stainless steel, but it's far from ideal from a galvanic point of view. When aluminum and stainless steel come in contact in the marine environment, a current flow is produced and the aluminum surrounding the screw will begin to corrode. Stainless screws in the aluminum mast need to be checked and, if necessary, replaced with new ones. A careful twist with a screwdriver will show you if the old screws need replacing. Re-tap the corroded aluminum and replace with larger screws. If the screws are frozen in aluminum oxide generated by the reaction, use a penetrating spray to help dissolve the corrosion freezing the stainless fastener. The best defense against galvanic corrosion is to insulate the new screws from the aluminum by wrapping them in protective MYLAR or TEFLON plumber's tape. For further protection, coat the screws with 3M POLYSULFIDE MARINE SEALANT 101. Spread some of the sealant and then rotate a screw through a hole in a piece of cardboard. The sealant will be forced into the threads of the screw. This approach of insulating dissimilar metals from one another should be followed with any dissimilar metals throughout the boat.

LANOCOTE anti-seize compound is often recommended for attaching fasteners to the mast. Screws coated with LANOCOTE will be less difficult to remove in the future. This is an anhydrous lanolin formula that makes a soft, nondrying barrier to corrosion. However, it probably does not do as good a job of preventing corrosion as do TEFLON tape and 3M POLYSULFIDE MARINE SEALANT 101.

### JAM CLEATS

Be sure that aluminum jam cleats have not clogged with dirt or become corroded. Each time you clean the deck, flush the cleats with generous quantities of water. A couple of times each season, squirt WD-40 on the movable parts, or rub them down with kerosene.

### PORT AND HATCH FRAMES

If a regular cleaning compound doesn't remove corrosion and stains from aluminum frames, again try 3M ALUMINUM RESTORER AND POLISH.

### STREAKED TOPSIDES

Water flowing over aluminum toerails is one cause of black streaks on the topsides. One Caribbean charter operator suggested coating the toerail with CORROSION X to remedy the problem.

## Stainless Steel

Steel contains iron, carbon, and any of a wide assortment of alloys. Steels made with the least carbon are more flexible and ductile, but not as strong as those with a higher carbon content. Most steels contain small amounts of alloys. In addition to carbon, nickel and manganese are added to increase steel's strength. For improved corrosion resistance, chromium or copper is added. For better machinability, lead or sulfur is added. For high-temperature performance, tungsten or molybdenum are alloyed to the steel. No matter what the use, the greater the amount of trace alloys, the more pronounced the desired effect.

For the marine industry, a strong steel with extremely good corrosion resistance is needed. Stainless steel fits this requirement perfectly. Marine stainless contains high quantities of chromium alloy and may contain quantities of nickel as well. The most corrosion-resistant marine parts are made of 316 stainless steel. Somewhat stronger, but with less corrosion resistance, is 304 stainless.

Although most people don't realize it, an oxidation phenomenon similar to that on aluminum occurs on stainless steel. In a process called passivation, the chromium alloy contained in stainless steel oxidizes on the surface and develops a corrosion-resistant protective film. When stainless is scratched, and the raw metal underneath is exposed, the chromium alloy oxidizes and a new protective oxide film forms on the scratch.

Stainless gets its excellent reputation by being a strong, highly corrosion-resistant metal. Nonetheless, parts made of stainless will eventually tarnish in a saltwater environment. It is often difficult to get at this tarnish unless you *carefully* use a cleaner containing some abrasives.

If a stainless part has routinely been kept tarnish-free, WINDEX is a good choice for general cleaning. For moderately stained stainless, try BAR

KEEPERS FRIEND (based on oxalic acid) or BON AMI (based on calcium carbonate, a mild abrasive). Both can be applied with a soft cloth or nylon scrubber. BAR KEEPERS FRIEND leaves a slightly greasy film on stainless that may help keep it from corroding. As always, no matter what cleaning agent you've used, rinse the part thoroughly with potable water after cleaning.

When stainless steel requires more serious cleaning and polishing, try 3M ONE STEP METAL RESTORER AND POLISH or T. L. SEA MARINE CLEANSER. Be careful not to overdo the rubbing, as too much polishing will scratch stainless. Rinse after cleaning.

For general corrosion protection, CRC HEAVY DUTY CORROSION INHIBITOR was the highest-rated corrosion-inhibiting product for stainless steel tested by *Practical Sailor* magazine in May 1998. The product differs from other sprays in that when the sprayed-on mist dries, it forms a rubbery protective film, not just an oily coating. It can also be used on electrical connections, engine components, and steering and throttle linkages, to name just a few.

CRC HEAVY DUTY CORROSION INHIBITOR also works well with discolored stainless-steel bolt and screw heads. Even after stainless heads begin to darken and show the first signs of corrosion, it is not too late to give them some protection. Lightly brush the heads with a bronze brush, clean with RUST OFF, rinse well after three minutes, and then spray on the CRC inhibitor for future protection.

Anhydrous lanolin, available in all drugstores, will prevent corrosion on almost any metal part. An important exception is any area—like battery terminals or engine components—where heat will soften the lanolin and make it run.

## Stainless Rigging Wire

For standing rigging, stainless-steel wire is almost without rival on modern recreational sailboats. Stainless wire rope is composed of strands wound around a core strand; each strand is itself composed of individual wires. The most popular strand arrangements are $1 \times 19$ and $7 \times 19$, where the first number refers to the number of strands and the second refers to the number of wires per strand. (In the case of $1 \times 19$, all the wires are the same size and the core wire is considered the sole strand.) When choosing stainless-steel wire, the main considerations are strength and flexibility. Composed of fewer wires, $1 \times 19$ is the strongest, but the least flexible. It is almost always used for standing rigging. As you would expect, $7 \times 19$ is more flexible but not as strong, although $7 \times 19$ might be seen as a wire halyard.

The table below gives the breaking strengths of the various types of stainless-steel rigging wire (for a ¼-inch gauge) commonly used on recreational sailboats. For comparison, I have also included values for Dacron double-braid line and Spectra core with a Dacron cover.

| MATERIAL | LAYUP | BREAKING STRENGTH |
|----------|-------|-------------------|
| Type 304 stainless | 1 × 19 | 8,200 lb. |
| Type 316 stainless | 1 × 19 | 7,090 lb. |
| Type 304 stainless | 7 × 19 | 6,400 lb. |
| Type 316 stainless | 7 × 19 | 5,040 lb. |
| Spectra core | Dacron cover | 4,300 lb. |
| Dacron | double braid | 1,800 lb. |

(Data source: Harken and West Marine catalogs.)

# Working with Metal

Most hardware stores sell cold chisels, blunt-ended heavy-duty chisels that cut metal when hit with a hammer. A cold chisel is often the best tool for general metal cutting and chipping, such as removing a bolt head or rivet. Like a pair of heavy-duty cable cutters, a cold chisel can be an essential on-board emergency tool.

If you are called upon to saw metal, first notch the starting point with a file. This will help the first sweep of the blade stay on target. Use sufficient pressure on the forward stroke to get the teeth to cut, then lift the saw slightly on the return stroke. For the best results, cut using the full length of the blade.

To cut metal tubing, put a snug-fitting piece of wood dowel inside the tube. The dowel will prevent the saw from snagging on the round edges as it cuts. To cut a flat piece, create a sandwich out of two wood pieces with the metal in between. Hold the piece tightly in the vise while you saw through the metal. Again, the wood will prevent the saw from snagging and will allow more precise cutting.

When filing the edge of a metal piece to remove a burr, always push the file away. Stroke up to make a beveled edge, which is called a radius. Don't use a naked file, as you will probably cut your hand. Either tape or put a handle on the file tang. A good filing job depends on choosing a file of the right size; use the wrong size and you will probably ruin the edge.

To create a hole in metal, start by drilling a pilot hole. If it is off-center—which always seems to happen to me—take a round-nosed cape chisel and cut a groove in the side of the hole where you would have preferred the drill to enter. This groove will pull the drill point in that direction and re-center the hole. Proceed slowly. If it is a hard metal, use a small drill first, and incrementally move up to the size drill you ultimately want. I use a variable-speed drill and generally begin at a slow speed.

Drill bits are made in an ascending order of quality and cost, beginning with nickel-alloyed steel bits, moving up to chromium, then to tungsten, and finally to cobalt. Cobalt bits will cut into stainless steel quite easily, and are capable of staying hard even when they get red hot. Like so many things, you get what you pay for. There are few things less satisfactory than trying to drill metal with a dull bit or a bit not suited to the job.

Eventually, you will be stumped by a disagreement between metric and U.S. Standard bits. There is a simple way to compare metric to U.S. Standard bits. If you know the millimeter size, multiply by 0.04 to get an approximate size in inches. When you know size in inches, multiply by 25.4 to get an approximation in millimeters.

Like any other metal part, rigging wire needs care. Corrosion will sometimes occur where the rigging wire enters a turnbuckle. Check the top end of the turnbuckles on a regular basis. To clean the wire, rub the wire with detergent, then with lacquer thinner. If necessary, abrade any corrosion off the wire using bronze wool, and rinse well. Spray the wire with a protective coating like CRC HEAVY DUTY CORROSION INHIBITOR at the point of entry into the turnbuckle. Finally, wipe the stainless wire thoroughly with WD-40. By getting a water-displacing penetrating oil onto and inside the wire shrouds, you will hopefully correct any problems affecting the wire's center and prevent future corrosion.

Few of us look under the vinyl chafe guards for problems. Vinyl chafe guards hold moisture inside that eventually causes mildew, algae, corrosion, and dirt to accumulate on the rigging wire. Remove the guards and follow the cleaning procedure above. Again, look particularly at the upper swaged end of the turnbuckle. After cleaning, consider leaving the chafe guards off. The rigging wires are likely to last longer out in the open where you can watch them than if they are hidden from view beneath shroud covers.

To clean wire rigging during the season, tie a rag soaked in detergent to the dirty shroud. Attach a halyard to the top and a long line to the bottom of the cloth. Pull the rag up with the halyard and down with the downhaul. When the mast is down at haulout time, you can easily reach and clean every inch of wire.

It's common practice to cover the cotter pins on turnbuckles with protective tape to prevent chafing. But tape traps moisture that eventually leads to corrosion. Instead, put a large bead of clear silicone, such as 3M MARINE GRADE MILDEW RESISTANT SILICONE, over the cotter pin ends to protect the pins from rust and the sails (and your ankles) from chafe.

## Winches

Not all winches are made of stainless steel, of course, but many are. Regardless of their composition, winches need regular care. Flush winches with potable water at the end of every outing in the boat. The potable water rinses away salt crystals and dirt that can abrade internal parts.

When you no longer hear a sharp clicking sound as the winch barrel turns, it is past time to replace the winch pawls, those metal cogs that control the braking action of the winch. Purchase a repair kit made for your specific winch. It will contain all the parts required for a maintenance upgrade.

When you disassemble a winch, put the parts in a bucket containing a few inches of gasoline or paint thinner. Use a toothbrush to scrub the pieces. Lay the clean parts out on clean cloth in the order of assembly. Putting all the pieces back together will then progress through a logical step-by-step process. Follow the winch manufacturer's lubrication suggestions exactly.

# Brass and Bronze

Brass and bronze are alloys based on copper—probably the world's oldest-known metal. Brass is an alloy of copper and zinc. Its color is determined by the percentage of zinc it contains, and ranges from reddish yellow to silvery yellow. Bronze is an alloy of copper and tin. It is harder than brass and much more expensive. Special bronze alloys are made with additional components such as aluminum, nickel, silicon, and phosphorous.

## Brass

Most brass is found below deck on clocks, barometers, sinks, and lamps. For general care, a mixture of white vinegar and salt (and elbow grease) will clean mildly tarnished brass quite well. Most decorative brass is polished and then coated with a lacquer (a clear finish similar to varnish) at the time of manufacture to prevent tarnishing. However, age and weather will tarnish even lacquered surfaces. To bring back the original finish, you must first remove the old lacquer. Use acetone or lacquer thinner and bronze wool along with vigorous scrubbing. These solvents will soften the lacquer finish, but are highly flammable and produce dangerous fumes, so be particularly careful in confined spaces. Remove the fine scratches the bronze wool made by buffing with NEVR-DULL POLISHING COTTON. Re-lacquering interior brass sinks or barometers will keep the shine lasting for a long time. Lacquer comes in aerosol form and is easy to spray on. On exterior brass, regular cleaning and polishing or waxing keeps corrosion away.

## Copper

The only copper you're likely to find on today's boats will be decorative. A mixture of white vinegar and salt will clean most tarnished copper. A commercial polish like NOXON 7 will spruce up lightly tarnished copper. As with other metals, a coat of wax or polymer polish will keep it shining much longer.

For routine cleaning, rub brass with a lemon dipped in salt. It does work—the British Navy relied on the salt-lemon solution for at least a century. For more serious cleaning, polish brass with a soft cloth with any one of three good cleaner/polishes: NOXON 7, NEVR-DULL, or FLITZ. For added protection, you might want to wipe on some petroleum jelly. It will leave a protective film that discourages tarnishing.

## Bronze

Bronze corrodes in a very obvious way. Upon exposure to water or a humid environment, the surface of a bronze part will oxidize and turn a harmless green that can be removed if it doesn't get too severe. Use NEVR-DULL for a slightly tarnished bronze surface; NOXON 7 (ammonia based) for a moderate tarnish; or T. L. SEA if you need some abrasive content to clean the surface.

### BRONZE PROPELLERS

When the boat is hauled out, carefully clean the propeller with an abrasive cleaner like BAR KEEPERS FRIEND until it shines, and then protect it with a

## Dealing with Corroded Fasteners

To help loosen rusted or corroded metals, use Liq-uid Wrench, white vinegar, or naval jelly. Scrub the part with a bronze wire brush to remove surface rust. If repeated applications of the penetrating substance fail to loosen the fastening, snap the rusted nut off by gripping it firmly with locking pliers and rocking back and forth until the metal breaks. Then, back the screw end off with a variable-speed power tool.

The Milwaukee Company, which manufactures heat guns, suggests you direct steady heat at rusted fasteners to loosen them. This is a good approach if care is taken not to damage any adjoining surfaces. If all else fails, use an impact wrench to remove a stubborn nut.

To prevent fasteners from seizing use Loc-tite #242 Removable Thread Locker, a compound that locks threaded parts and prevents them from loosening, yet permits easy disassembly when required.

A fairly new product, Star brite Corrosion Buster Pen is unique in its ability to clean tiny crevices on stainless steel hardware and in the grooves of fastenings. Try this product when other abrasive products can't get at the accumulations of rust, dirt, grease, wax, or paint in tight spots. There are approximately 20,000 very fine glass fibers in the tip of the corrosion buster pen that don't scratch. Adjusting the bristles to short lengths helps them work better on heavy-duty projects. I'm sure the pen will become a hot item for immaculate boaters.

coating of STP Oil Treatment or bronze polish. Nothing will last long on the prop, but by keeping it smooth and clean, barnacles and grime will have a harder time settling. Some boaters swear that spraying lacquer onto a clean prop works for a whole season. On & Off will loosen barnacle rings and zebra mussels from the prop.

BRONZE SEACOCKS

Check seacocks often for slow leaks and corrosion and to assure easy lever movement. A stuck seacock is never acceptable, so use a marine grease like white lithium grease to keep the valves operating smoothly. A film of CRC Heavy Duty Corrosion Inhibitor sprayed on the surface gives some added corrosion protection to a seacock.

## Placing Difficult Screws

It is often difficult to hold a screw in place when the spot is hard to reach. Tape the screw to the tip of the screwdriver. It will now be easy to point the screw into the hole and twist it in with the screwdriver.

## Chrome

To produce the bright, shiny surface we prize in chrome, manufacturers use a process called electrodisposition that adds a thin layer of chromium to a base metal of bronze, brass, or steel. This layer of chrome also protects the base metals. A well-deposited chrome layer is impervious to attack from most chemicals, except muriatic and sulfuric acid. (If you find pits in

4

## Emergency Tip: Fouled Props

If you have to cut a line that has fouled your prop, try fastening a serrated knife to a boathook with hose clamps. You should be able to saw through the line from the dinghy or the deck and avoid an unscheduled swim. Hope springs eternal.

chrome, acid rain may be the cause.) To keep pitting from starting on chrome parts, clean them frequently with an alcohol-based window cleaner like WINDEX. It works well on chrome deck hinges, pulpits, and engine controls. Use a wax or polish after cleaning.

Use FLITZ or NEVR-DULL to polish moderately tarnished chrome. If there has been more serious heat discoloration, as often occurs with chromed exhaust pipes, warm the surface and apply FLITZ. Wait for three minutes, then rub briskly with a soft towel.

3M ULTRA PERFORMANCE PASTE WAX does a good job of waxing chrome.

If you keep your boat in an urban or industrial area, every rainfall is probably coating it with a variety of airborne acidic chemicals. After every rainstorm, and whenever you wash down the deck, wipe all chrome parts with a pseudo-chamois cloth to prevent spotting and eventual pitting. Synthetic chamois cloths are available at automotive stores. Chamois is high on my list of indispensable boat-cleaning supplies.

# Iron and Nonstainless Steel

Cast iron is often used in sailboat keels. Due to their high carbon content, iron castings are strong, hard, and brittle. Wrought iron, on the other hand, contains almost no carbon and, unless specially treated, is so brittle it becomes nearly useless. (That, incidentally, is why you won't see it on boats.) Nonstainless steel is commonly used for anchor chain.

## Chain

Steel anchor chain is widely available in three grades.

> **Proof coil** is a strong, low-carbon chain popular with recreational boaters, but its long links do not fit well on anchor windlasses.

> **BBB chain** is another low-carbon steel chain with shorter links that ride over a windlass properly.

> **High-test chain** is made of a high-carbon steel that is lighter for the same strength, making it ideal for those who want to reduce weight at the bow.

All three grades of chain are usually galvanized, or coated with a thin layer of zinc, for protection against rust. In addition, there is 316 stainless steel chain for those who desire extraordinary corrosion resistance.

What to do with rusted chain? Sandblasting, followed by a commercial dip in hot zinc can often rejuvenate severely rusted steel chain. For a do-it-yourself project with a moderately affected chain, clean as much rust off as possible with a wire brush, flake the chain out on the dock on top of a plastic tarp. Spray-paint the chain with CRC INSTANT GALVANIZE, a product containing zinc dust and toluol. Its zinc-rich formula protects clean, previously galvanized metal. It renews and repairs most galvanized surfaces. I've even heard that heavy equipment operators drag lengths of chain on concrete highways. The friction cleans off rust almost as well as sandblasting. To clean smaller steel parts that have rusted, buff them with a knotted wire wheel on a four-inch, 10,000 rpm grinder.

### SANDBLASTING IRON KEELS

The keel of a sailboat is the only place you're likely to find iron. When external iron keels develop severe rust, they must be sandblasted clean. After sandblasting, the voids should be filled with a high-quality epoxy. Epoxy is expensive and difficult to sand, but it holds up better than any other product. Inexpensive polyester automotive body fillers, for example, are easy to sand but will not last like epoxy.

If there are only isolated rust spots, chip off flaking metal, wire-brush the rusty metal, and then apply a rust-preventing primer like OSPHO, which is available at automotive stores. The phosphoric acid in OSPHO converts the rust (iron oxide) to a nonrust product (iron phosphate.) The clear primer turns black when it dries. A bottom paint can now be applied.

Zinc phosphate spray metal primers are available at marine stores and can also do an adequate job of priming bare, shiny metal spots. Fair the indentation with an epoxy and then apply bottom paint.

## Metal Filings

After you've drilled into metal, there will be thousands of tiny metal shavings blowing all over. They are sharp, so don't try scooping them up with your hands. Take a large piece of the widest box-sealing tape you can find and pat it into the shavings. Most of them will stick to the tape. You might even lay the tape, sticky side up, around the perimeter of the work site before you begin.

## Metal-Cleaning Kit

I've found it helpful to create a simple metal-cleaning kit. I buy a few basic cleaners and polishes that work on most metal surfaces and keep them together in a cleaning bucket. A starting list might include WD-40, FANTASTIK, WINDEX, BON AMI, 3M ONE STEP METAL RESTORER AND POLISH, FLITZ, petroleum jelly, bronze wool, rags, pseudo-chamois, and wire brushes. You'll be surprised at the number of problems these few products will cure.

## Cleaning the Engine

A clean engine works better, smells better, and looks better. Grease and oil can hide problems that are easily seen on a clean engine. Furthermore, smoke and fumes will come off a hot, dirty engine.

CRC CLEANER AND DEGREASER aerosol dissolves grease and oil. Protect electrical connections and air intakes before you spray it on the engine and let it stand for the required time. Hose off when the product has completed its job. A clean engine is the reward.

Here's a way to lessen the mess of removing oil from the engine. On inboard engines, many boaters use a brass piston-style pump to remove oil through the dipstick hole. But, invariably, the hose you put down the dipstick hole is too small and it will pop out and spew oil in every direction. To prevent this, remove the flexible hose at the adapter near the pump handle. Replace this piece of hose with about two feet of copper tubing with a diameter that will fit snugly into the dipstick hole. A piece of quarter-inch copper tube will probably be the right size. At the discharge end, put the hose in the neck of a plastic milk jug. It's a convenient container to carry used oil to the gas station for proper disposal. When you've finished removing the oil, put the oil-removal pump in a big ZIPLOC bag, along with a wad of paper toweling, for clean storage. Otherwise, oil will seep out of the hose and pump and make a mess of wherever the unit is stored.

You can also make the job of changing the oil filter a little less messy by putting a plastic bag around the filter before you twist it off. The bag will catch and hold most of the oil that would otherwise spill into the bilge. If you can't get the filter to twist off, plunge a long screwdriver into the old filter and use it as a lever to turn the filter counterclockwise.

# Quick-Reference Guide
## Metal

| MATERIAL | TOPIC | JOB | PAGE | PRODUCT | HOW TO DO JOB |
|---|---|---|---|---|---|
| **Aluminum** | | Surface dirt | 41 | **BOAT ZOAP** | Wet surface with dilute **BOAT ZOAP**. Rinse. |
| | Winch housing | Chalky surface | 41 | **3M "ONE STEP" RESTORER AND POLISH; WEST MARINE METAL POLISH** | Polish with clean cloth and rinse. |
| | Mast screws | Corroded | 41 | **TEFLON** tape; **3M POLYSULFIDE MARINE SEALANT 101; LANOCOTE** | Insulate screws from galvanic activity with **TEFLON** tape or **101**. Coat with **LANOCOTE** for easy removal. |
| | Jam cleats | Dirty | 42 | Water; **WD-40**; kerosene | Flush with water. Apply **WD-40** or kerosene |
| | Hatch frame | Dirty | 42 | **3M "ONE STEP" ALUMINUM RESTORER AND POLISH** | Wipe on and buff. |
| | Toerails | Black streaks | 42 | **CORROSION X** | Coat toerail with **CORROSION X** to prevent black steaks on topsides. |
| **Stainless steel** | | Mild soil | 42 | **WINDEX** | Spray on. Wipe dry. |
| | | Moderate soil | 42–43 | **BAR KEEPERS FRIEND; BON AMI** | Apply with soft cloth. Rinse. |
| | | Severe soiling | 43 | **3M "ONE STEP" METAL RESTORER AND POLISH; T. L. SEA MARINE CLEANSER** | Apply with soft cloth. Rub carefully, don't scratch. Rinse. Apply a marine polish for protection. |
| | Screw heads | Rusty | 43 | **RUST OFF; CRC HEAVY DUTY CORROSION INHIBITOR** | Paint screw heads with diluted **RUST OFF**. Rinse after 3 minutes. Spray on **CRC CORROSION INHIBITOR**. |
| | Turnbuckle | Corrosion protection | 45 | **CRC HEAVY DUTY CORROSION INHIBITOR** | Wash. Scrub with cleaner. Apply **CRC INHIBITOR** to protect surface. |

*continues*

# Quick-Reference Guide

## Metal (continued)

| MATERIAL | TOPIC | JOB | PAGE | PRODUCT | HOW TO DO JOB |
|---|---|---|---|---|---|
| **Stainless steel, ctd.** | Rigging wire | Dirty | 45 | **WD-40;** lacquer thinner | Wipe with lacquer thinner. Wash with detergent. Rinse. Wipe **WD-40** on wire. |
| | Cotter pins | Preventing chafing | 45 | **3M MARINE GRADE MILDEWRESISTANT SILICONE** | Remove conventional tape from cotter pins. Spray silicone on sharp ends. |
| **Copper** | Ornament | Tarnished | 46 | White vinegar and salt; **NOXON 7** | Apply solution. Polish with soft cloth. |
| **Brass** | Barometer | Mild tarnish | 46 | White vinegar and salt; or lemon dipped in salt | Apply solution. Polish with soft cloth. |
| | Lamp | Tarnished | 46 | **FLITZ; NEVR-DULL** | Polish with soft cloth while polish still wet. |
| **Bronze** | Propeller | Slightly dirty | 46 | **NEVR-DULL** | Wipe surface with saturated cloth. |
| | | Heavy soil | 46 | **NOXON 7; BAR KEEPERS FRIEND; T. L. SEA MARINE CLEANSER** | Clean. Polish. Rinse. Apply **STP OIL TREATMENT** for future protection. |
| | Seacock | Slight corrosion | 47 | **CRC HEAVY DUTY CORROSION INHIBITOR** | Clean. Spray on inhibitor for corrosion protection. |
| **Chrome** | Compass mount | Dirty | 48 | **WINDEX** | Spray on. Rinse. Chamois dry. |
| | Engine control lever | Corroded | 48 | **FLITZ; NEVR-DULL; 3M ULTRA PERFORMANCE PASTE WAX** | Clean. Polish. Rinse. Apply wax for protection. Buff. |
| **Steel** | Chain | Rusted | 49 | **CRC INSTANT GALVANIZE** | Sandblast. Spray on **CRC** paint. |
| **Iron** | Keel | Rusted | 49 | **OSPHO** | Chip. Wire brush. Apply **OSPHO**. Fair smooth. Apply bottom paint. |

# 5

# SELECTION AND
# APPLICATION
# OF COATINGS

The marine environment will quickly degrade the color, finish, or corrosion resistance you have labored to produce on your boat. Paints, varnishes, and other coatings play a critical role in boat maintenance. The right coating will often protect and beautify simultaneously. Coatings can preserve and even enhance the value of your boat. Nonetheless, I'm still amazed at the sheer volume written about coatings, and the anxiety that paints and other coatings inspire in many boaters. It's a complex subject, but if we proceed logically and carefully, the clouds will soon lift.

Your goals will dictate the choice of coating. The first steps are always to decide what you wish to accomplish, the scope of the job, and the timing. I strongly recommend that, as your next step, you go to a marine store and ask for the paint specialist. In my experience, every marine store has at least one person who enjoys talking about paint. Pick his or her brain. Ask about anything you don't understand. Once you have narrowed the choice down to a specific type and brand, read the label carefully. The manufacturers have put their entire experience with this product on the back of the can. If there was ever a time to read the instructions, this is it. Don't assume all paints are alike. Each formulation may require a different thinner, a different primer, or specific drying times between coats. Follow the instructions on the label to the letter. Ask for the paint manufacturer's informational pamphlet. They all produce one, and your marine store should have them for distribution. The pamphlets normally contain very general information but they are helpful for translating the technical jargon into layman's language. Last, but not least, boating magazines often review specific marine coatings and make recommendations.

In theory, if you follow these steps no coating project should be beyond your ability. Perhaps you are already objecting: this is what you've done for years—with mixed results. You're still baffled by the dozens of competing, seemingly identical products. If so, don't despair. In this chapter,

I'll explain marine coatings in layman's terms. I'll begin with the simplest definition of a coating and work toward a fuller explanation of the processes involved as the chapter progresses. The opening sections of the chapter present the essential information on coating projects. The latter sections address specific surfaces to be coated.

# Coating Basics

## Coating Components

Almost all coatings are composed of three parts.

- ▶ Resin, which is the glue that holds the coating together.

- ▶ Pigment, which adds color, thickness, or protection from sunlight.

- ▶ Additives that serve a specific function. Typical paint additives make the coating flow better, affect the drying time, or resist destructive ultraviolet rays.

Each of the three main ingredients of a coating has an important job, and most coatings would fail without any one. (An exception is varnish, which contains no pigment.)

These three basic components are milled together by the manufacturer and put in a can. Because of the enormous variety of end uses, application methods, and local climate, the paint manufacturers make their products as all-purpose and "idiot-proof" as possible. And in composing the instructions on the label, they make every effort to steer the user to a successful result.

There are, however, two variables over which the manufacturer has no control: the condition of the surface to be painted, and the weather. It's your responsibility to follow the manufacturer's advice.

### RESIN

The resin is the heart of any coating. It is also called the binder, and that is exactly what it does. It binds all the ingredients together and bonds the coating to the substrate (the underlying surface). Natural resins like tung oil or linseed oil have been around for as long as anyone can remember, and have their fanatic advocates. Synthetic resins came into their own around the time of World War II, and have brought improvements over natural resins in color, resistance to ultraviolet rays, shelf life, and longevity. Polyurethane and epoxy are examples of synthetic resins. Whether it's synthetic or natural, a resin's purpose is literally to wrap around the pigment and additives and hold them in suspension, not unlike the way gelatin supports fruit. It must keep them in place until the system dries or cures. As it cures, the resin hardens and grips the properly prepared surface below with a tenacious chemical bond. However, if the surface is dirty, shiny, or contains wax, the binder will not find the nooks and crannies it needs to grip to form a successful chemical attachment. The result is a weak mechanical bond that will sooner or later let go. *Poor surface preparation is probably the number one cause of paint failure.*

## PIGMENT

The pigments are the next important component in most coatings. Titanium dioxide is added to make the paint white. Cuprous oxide lends toxicity to antifouling paints that kill marine growth. Synthetic and natural pigments are included to give the paint color. Finely ground fillers are often added to improve paint performance. All of these products begin as dry powders that are milled into the resin along with the additives. During the milling process, the binder wets the pigments, as you do when you mix cocoa with milk to make hot chocolate. However, pigments are heavier than the other ingredients in coatings. (Cuprous oxide, for example, is extremely heavy and quickly sinks to the bottom of the can.) All pigments tend to settle, which is why paints must be stirred before use, to get the ingredients back into suspension.

## ADDITIVES

Additives are put into the paint to assist the other two ingredients to do their job. All paints contain some additives. Naturally, the manufacturer has an interest in producing a product that can be used anywhere in the country. Additives allow manufacturers to produce paints that will function reasonably well across a wide range of climates and environments. Nonetheless, one paint can't do everything. This is the primary reason why paint manufacturers make different products for the same purpose, and this is where the customer confusion begins. A manufacturer might offer a line of between four and six different bottom paints. Each exists for a specific use or method of application. Choosing among them is where a little education comes in handy.

## Marine Coatings

At the microscopic level, all coatings will look more or less the same. Think of them as sandwiches.

All coatings will look much like a cut-away section of a paint film (see fig. 5-1 next page). You are looking at a highly magnified cross section of a layer of paint, not unlike a side view of a sandwich cut in half.

The top of the paint film is a resin-rich area that is exposed to the weather. Dispersed through the middle of the paint sandwich are pigment agglomerates embedded or encased in resin. The bottom of the film is resin, tightly gripping the wood substrate. A side view of gelcoat would look very similar to this, with gelcoat adhering to a fiberglass base. Varnish will look somewhat different, in that it generally has no pigment, and will be all resin. Bottom paints will show a great amount of pigment dispersed in the film.

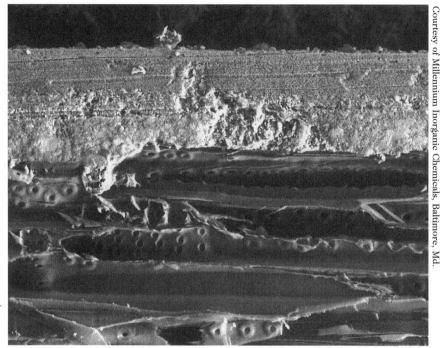

Courtesy of Millennium Inorganic Chemicals, Baltimore, Md.

*Figure 5-1. Side view of a paint film, magnified 200 times.*

These before-and-after electron-micrograph photos of a paint film (figs. 5-2 and 5-3) dramatically illustrate what happens to paint or gelcoat when it weathers.

Figure 5-2 is an overhead view of the exposed surface of a new paint film. Clumps of pigment particles are embedded in hazy resin.

Figure 5-3 illustrates what happens when paint or gelcoat weathers. On exposure to the elements, the resin-rich top surface wears away, leaving pigment particles out in the open. The hazy resin we saw in figure 5-2 has worn off, or weathered, leaving bare pigment particles exposed. Without the protection of the glossy surrounding resin, the surface of the film will appear dull and chalky and soon the pigment particles will lose their grip and wear off. These particles, no longer held in place by resin, form the dull surface you see on oxidized fiberglass and chalking paint.

Gelcoat shares the same components as paint—resin, pigment, and additives—and the process of deterioration is much the same: a once-glossy finish becomes dull, and eventually chalky, as more loose pigment is exposed.

Below, you will find a list of commonly used marine paints and coatings. To approach the topic in the most sensible way, I have organized the list and rest of this chapter around surfaces to be coated. Each surface will be discussed in detail: how to prepare the substrate, what type of coating to use, and how to apply it. Look up the surface you want to

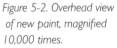

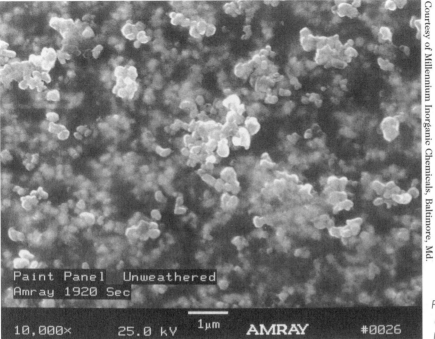

Courtesy of Millennium Inorganic Chemicals, Baltimore, Md.

Figure 5-2. Overhead view of new paint, magnified 10,000 times.

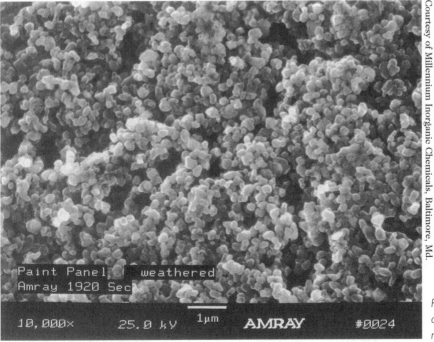

Courtesy of Millennium Inorganic Chemicals, Baltimore, Md.

Figure 5-3. Overhead view of weathered paint, magnified 10,000 times.

coat and follow the steps. When applicable, I will add specific product recommendations.

FIBERGLASS BOTTOMS

- ▶ Epoxy or vinylester barrier coats (to prevent moisture from penetrating the gelcoat)
- ▶ Soft antifouling paints
- ▶ Hard copolymer antifouling paints
- ▶ Ablative antifouling paints
- ▶ Teflon antifouling paints
- ▶ Water-based antifouling paints
- ▶ Aluminum antifouling paints
- ▶ Outboard, and inboard/outboard coatings

FIBERGLASS TOPSIDES AND DECK

- ▶ One-component polyurethane paints
- ▶ Two-component polyurethane paints
- ▶ Conventional alkyd enamels
- ▶ Accent paints and graphics
- ▶ Nonskid coatings

WOOD

- ▶ Topside paints
- ▶ Conventional tung-oil varnish
- ▶ Polyurethane varnish
- ▶ Teak treatments

INTERIOR

- ▶ Interior varnish
- ▶ Enamels
- ▶ Polyurethanes

# The Successful Coating Project

There are three steps to a successful project: preparation, selection, and application.

## *Preparation*

Before any painting can begin, the underlying surface must be prepared so that the coating can adhere to it. Surface preparation is the hard and dirty part of a coating project. But nothing affects the final outcome more. If you do not take the time here, coating failure is all but certain. For every hour you spend actually painting, you may well spend eight hours getting the surface ready. If for no other reason, the long hours of preparation should induce you to buy the best and longest-lasting paint available.

The goal of preparation is to create what paint professionals call "tooth." No new paint can adhere for long to a surface that is dirty, greasy, or waxy. A successful paint or varnish job requires a clean, roughened surface that the coating likes and can get a good grip on. Of course, good adhesion to an unsound substrate—say, an earlier coating that itself lacks good adhesion—is no better.

Surface preparation will always include cleaning, degreasing, and sanding. Priming is often required as well. Primers are preliminary coatings used as "mediators" when the topcoat is unlikely to adhere to the substrate. Primers adhere tenaciously to the substrate and in turn offer the topcoat a good "tooth." In some cases, preparation may even mean sandblasting.

## Selection

Why buy cheap paint? It is more likely to fail, and when it does, you will be forced to duplicate all the hard work you put into preparation. The best paint is more expensive, and it is for a reason. High-quality paints use the best possible raw materials and are generally formulated to last longer. You almost always get what you pay for with paint.

In a number of cases below, I have recommended specific products made by INTERLUX, PETTIT, or WOOLSEY. I do not mean to imply that paints made by other manufacturers are not equally good. It is simply not possible to compare paint products exhaustively within the scope of this book. Unlike most other cleaning and maintenance products, paints are manufactured to do very specific jobs. Each major manufacturer has designed a paint for a given purpose. Competing paints within a specific category, say ablative bottom coatings, tend to have similar performance. Occasionally, a manufacturer comes out with an outstanding product, but this is very difficult to quantify or prove. As I've said, your first concerns should be identifying the correct *type* of paint for the job, preparing the surface properly, and applying the paint as directed.

So which paint should you buy? Read this chapter carefully. Then talk to other boat owners in your area. Find out what has worked for them. Talk to an expert at the marine store. Tell him or her what coating is on the boat now. Describe the condition of the surface you wish to cover. Describe how and where the boat is moored. Read the product reviews in the boating magazines. Consult the informational brochures put out by the manufacturers themselves. As you gain experience, personal preference will become a factor. For complex projects involving a number of different products, I would suggest that you choose a product line and then stick to the manufacturer's system to simplify the process and avoid tricky compatibility issues. For example, if you plan to use a polyurethane topside paint by

Brand X, the safer bet is to use the Brand X fairing compound, primers, and solvents as well.

Don't try to thin the paint out to make it go further. Unless the label specifically calls for thinning, it has been formulated at the correct consistency. Always get a little more than you think you need, as there will always be spills and touchups. Keep a record of what you used, so that next year, when the can has been discarded, you will know what to buy.

## Application

Once the surface has been prepared and the paint has been chosen, the easiest part of the job remains—applying the coating. This is where you receive the most satisfaction. Watching a pale piece of wood burst into life with a coat of varnish, or a mottled bottom become like new, is a source of immense pleasure. Once again, read the label on the can carefully for limits on temperature and timing, and hints on how to apply the coating. Follow these instructions if at all possible.

Many coating projects call for good timing and choreography. Varnishing requires the application of up to eight coats before you are done. You will be forced to bet on the temperature holding steady, and to hope that no wind kicks up midway and blows dust into the wet varnish. If you are applying a barrier coat—a waterproof paint used to seal the hull—you will find that the drying times allowed between each of the several coatings are very precise. You may be at it for a whole weekend, and you'll have to plan ahead for the best possible weather. (And always allow some extra time for the inevitable frantic trip to the marine store.)

In general, whenever a manufacturer provides a recoating schedule that you must follow, it is to ensure that a chemical bond, and not merely a mechanical bond, is created between the coats. If the instructions require that you recoat before the paint has cured, the manufacturer wants the new layer to use its solvents to soften the preceding layer to get a good bite and create a chemical bond. If the paint is allowed to cure and harden, the new layer may not be able to soften the old layer. It will only create a mechanical bond that will eventually fail.

Don't ignore the safety cautions. Most of us never read them. Some coatings contain extremely toxic ingredients. Wear safety goggles, protective clothing, gloves, and breathing devices if suggested.

Wipe the surface down as recommended before you put the roller in the pan. Sanding is not enough. Most coatings require a solvent wash and/or a wipedown with a tack cloth before painting.

In the end, a good paint job depends on the painter. It is up to you to choose the proper weather conditions, prepare the surface properly, mix the coating as directed, apply the right amount of coating, and insure adequate drying time before launching the boat.

## The Painting Tool Kit

Keep the following items in a convenient place where the hazards of storing flammable chemicals (solvents) can be minimized.

- A few 1-inch and 3-inch disposable foam brushes
- A couple of hog bristle disposable brushes
- A couple of 1-inch and a 2-inch China bristle brushes
- A 9-inch roller pan that can be lined with kitchen plastic wrap and used over and over

- Solvent-resistant rollers
- Acetone and mineral spirits (one quart each)
- Chemical-resistant gloves
- Wooden paint mixers
- A metal mixing attachment to be used with a power tool for mixing heavily settled paint

Put these items in a couple of nested disposable cardboard pails and everything will be at your fingertips when you are ready to paint.

I offer the recommendations that follow as good generalizations based on products and procedures that have gained acceptance within the industry. If my suggestions should disagree with the manufacturer's instructions, follow the instructions on the can. Don't be intimidated by a painting project, or by the number of recommendations in this chapter. You'll only be tackling one project at a time. Find that project in the following paragraphs and choose a good day to put the brush in the can. Before you know it, you will be standing back and smiling at a job well done.

The table on page 62 compares similar paints made by different manufacturers. Each paint will have its adherents, as there will be slight differences in their application or final result. This table is meant to give you a generic reference when comparing related paints.

## Bare Fiberglass Bottom

You may have occasion to apply antifouling paint to a bare fiberglass bottom: with a new boat; with a sound hull stripped of an excessive buildup of previous bottom coats; or with a freshwater boat that has been moved to salt water. This is often an opportune time to apply a barrier coat to improve the hull's resistance to moisture and head off problems with osmotic blisters.

# Paint Comparison Chart

| | INTERLUX | WOOLSEY | PETTIT | OTHERS |
|---|---|---|---|---|
| **Primers** | | | | |
| Fiberglass primer | AL200 | | 6999 | |
| Aluminum primer | 353/354 | | METAL PRIMER | |
| **Fillers** | | | | |
| Epoxy | 417A/418B | GOLD PRIMER | FLEXBOND | |
| Fairing compound | V135A/136A | | 7020/7025 | |
| **Barrier coats** | | | | |
| Fiberglass | 1000/1001 | | | WEST SYSTEM |
| | 2000/2001 | GOLD | | WEST SYSTEM WITH BARRIER ADDITIVE |
| Aluminum | 404/414 | | FLEXBOND | |
| **Bottom paints** | | | | |
| Fiberglass | | | | |
| Modified epoxy | ULTRA-KOTE | NEPTUNE | TRINIDAD | |
| ablative single-season | ACT | | | |
| ablative multiseason | MICRON CSC | | ACP50 | |
| Aluminum | TRI-LUX II | | | |
| **Topside paints** | | | | |
| Polyurethane, single-part | BRIGHTSIDE | MIRACOTE | EASYPOXY | |
| Nonskid additive | NOSKID 2398 | NON-SKID COMPOUND | | |
| **Bilge paint** | BILGEKOTE 863 | | POLYPOXY | |
| **Varnish** | | | | |
| Tung oil | SCHOONER | | EASYPOXY HI-BUILD | EPIFANES GLOSS |
| Polyurethane | CLIPPER | | ULTRA V-GOLD | EPIFANE MATTE |
| Synthetic | | | | CETOL |

# Antifouling Paints

Federal legislation has banned the use of tin-based bottom paints as too toxic for general use. This has caused most bottom-paint manufacturers to switch to antifouling paints based on cuprous oxide, a powdered form of copper that is less toxic than tin. Recently, there has been a concerted effort to market water-based bottom paints that do not release harmful solvents into the atmosphere as they dry. These paints are still based on copper, and behave like conventional paints under water.

Selecting a bottom paint can be confusing. Narrow the field, based on your boating and your personal criteria. Consider the following:

- What type of water will the boat operate in? Freshwater, brackish water, salt water, or tropical water?

- What type of boat is involved? Sailboat, powerboat, high-performance craft, workboat, dinghy?

- Is cost an important factor?

- How often is the boat used? Full-year, seasonal, trailered?

Most manufacturers produce a line of bottom paint for severe fouling to be used in tropical waters. It will be heavily loaded with the toxic agent, cuprous oxide. They will also produce a line for moderately foul areas, with a different formulation and less cuprous oxide, that will be appropriate for an area like the Chesapeake Bay. Freshwater boaters have their choice of almost any product, as the fouling on their boats will be low. However, the amount of cuprous oxide required in your area is only one factor. The cruising speed of your boat is another. At high speeds, an ablative paint will wear off rapidly; a speedboat owner should look at a hard, high-gloss Teflon or vinyl bottom paint. If expense is no object, go for the paint with the highest cuprous content and you'll run the least risk of your bottom fouling with marine growth. The argument for inexpensive bottom paints is not too strong. Expensive paints are normally formulated to last longer, so the lower initial cost may well be offset by the need to repaint sooner. Specialty paints are available for aluminum bottoms.

Of course, trailered boats will rarely use bottom paint as there is little opportunity for marine growth to adhere, plus bottom paints will scrape off as the boat is loaded and unloaded from the trailer.

Once you have a picture of what you need, you can decide which of the many types of antifouling paint to purchase. These are the most common types:

## MODIFIED EPOXY

These are one-part epoxy paints that dry to a hard finish, which can be scrubbed. They are often described as "hard paints." The toxic ingredient, cuprous oxide, leaches out, leaving the resin on the hull. A cross section of a fully depleted, hard, bottom paint would look like a sponge. They can be applied on top of almost any other hard paint. Succeeding layers of paint

# Haul-Out Hints

If your boat will be hauled out on slings when the time comes for a new coat of antifouling paint, you'll need to be certain the slings are correctly placed, otherwise they could damage a rudder, an impeller, a propeller shaft, or an underwater fitting.

Photograph the boat from all sides when it's hauled out. In your photo, include some above-the-waterline reference point such as the forward stays or a porthole. The next time the boat is hauled, the yard people can refer to the photographs for sling positioning.

New boats often have small "sling" stickers placed at the strap points by the manufacturer. These stickers can easily be made from a label gun and applied to your boat.

Photos will also help to locate the position of a through-hull if, in an emergency, you must go over the side to plug a leak.

At haulout time, you will probably be going up and down a ladder for the hundred tasks that must be done in a short time. Tie pieces of carpet or towels on the first two rungs of the ladder. As you step on the carpet, most of the yard dirt from your shoes will be left behind. Place a synthetic grass mat on the deck at the top of the ladder as the last protection to keep the boat clean.

build up and must eventually be removed. They are good for boats that stay in the water all the time.

### ABLATIVE

These are based on copolymer resins that erode away at a controlled rate and carry the toxic ingredient with it. The paint will be gone at the end of its programmed lifetime. Burnishing is not recommended, although racers sometimes do it. (In normal application, ablatives are not smooth enough for racing.) Some higher-end brands can be relaunched for multiple seasons without the need for sanding and repainting. In general, ablative bottom paints are popular with boaters who haul their boats at the end of the season and plan to recoat in the spring.

### TEFLON

These smooth, very thin finishes are mostly used on high-performance powerboats and racing sailboats. They dry quickly to a slick finish. Users must be careful that the paint has not lost its effectiveness when the boat is relaunched after being out of the water. It will soon become obvious that the paint is no longer effective if marine growth begins on the bottom.

### VINYL

These paints can be burnished to a slick finish, and provide a low-friction hull, but are not compatible with most other bottom coatings. They are primarily used on high-performance boats.

### SLOUGHING PAINTS

These are inexpensive, soft, rough-surfaced, one-season paints that are gone at the end of the season. They are used frequently by workboats, as slime

# Aluminum under Water

Aluminum is commonly used for dinghies and components of outboards and sterndrives. As we saw in chapter 4, when aluminum is scratched, the outer oxide layer will form again and protect the surface. A mast will rarely need a coating, but dinghy bottoms and underwater components of engines are often primed and painted. You should never use a conventional, cuprous oxide-based bottom paint on aluminum as the cuprous oxide will create a galvanic reaction with the aluminum that will negate the protection of the copper. Instead, use bottom paints specially formulated for aluminum. Standard procedure for bottom-coating aluminum is as follows.

Clean the surface with a solvent wash. If the surface is especially foul, sandblast, or use a medium-grit emery cloth to bring the aluminum to a bright surface. Clean the area again. Prime the clean metal surface with an aluminum primer such as INTERLUX VINY-LUX PRIMEWASH 353/354 or PETTIT METAL PRIMER. Apply at least two coats of an aluminum antifouling paint.

It's a challenge to get good paint performance on outboards and sterndrive units. The vibration, abrasion, and turbulence doom most finishes to early failure. (Aluminum is often used for these components so, again, do not use cuprous oxide-based antifouling paints.)

To paint a lower unit, first clean it thoroughly. Sand the old paint with 80-grit sandpaper. Sand bare metal with a coarse emery cloth. Then clean again. Prime using an underwater primer (INTERLUX VINY-LUX PRIMEWASH 353/354 or PETTIT METAL PRIMER will serve here too). Follow this with two or three coats of either an aerosol primer like the INTERLUX TRI-LUX II AEROSOL KIT or, if you want to use a brush, an underwater primer such as INTERLUX UNDERWATER PRIMER 360. Apply up to three coats of an aluminum antifouling paint.

INTERLUX VINY-LUX PRIMEWASH 353/354 or PETTIT METAL PRIMER will also allow you to paint underwater bronze, such as through-hull fittings, and other metals. Clean the surface thoroughly with a solvent wash. Apply a very thin coat of the primer, and then proceed with barrier or antifouling coats.

---

and barnacles will leave with the paint. They are designed to flake off, rather than wearing away like an ablative paint. Once applied, they must be removed before a harder paint can be used.

### ALUMINUM PAINTS

Paints for aluminum bottoms are specially formulated without cuprous oxide because the close proximity of aluminum and copper would set up a galvanic reaction and lead to corrosion.

## Barrier Coats

If you find yourself gazing at a pristine unpainted bottom, seriously consider applying a barrier coat. Again, this would occur either with a boat whose bottom had never been painted (a boat used in freshwater, or a new boat) or a hull stripped clean of previous coats of bottom paint. A barrier coat is a specially formulated paint, based on epoxy or vinylester, designed to resist water penetration better than the boat's gelcoat. Barrier coats are most commonly used to repair and prevent osmotic blistering (see page 66). By

# Osmotic Blisters

If water penetrates the gelcoat and encounters water-soluble material in the laminate, such as a pocket of uncured resin, a reaction will occur that draws more water in. The result is a blister of acidic fluid under pressure that will eventually break the surface. A few blisters are not the end of the world, and many boatowners undertake repairs themselves, following the general approach I describe below. If the underside of the boat is literally covered with blisters, the condition is far more serious, and the gelcoat may have to be removed entirely below the waterline to allow the hull to dry. Such a project is beyond the scope of this book.

The first step is to open the blister. Be sure to wear eye protection, as the fluid may erupt with some force. Grind out the crater with a disk sander to create a shallow, beveled surface suitable for bonding. Clean the opening well.

The hull must then be allowed to dry thoroughly. This will often require the boat to be out of the water for months. A hull will dry most rapidly if stored indoors with heating and good air circulation. Use a moisture meter (your yard should have one) to determine if the opened blisters are dry. When the bottom-moisture readings above and below the waterline are the same, work may proceed.

Wipe the repair area with the recommended solvent. First paint the repair with an epoxy such as INTERLUX INTERPROTECT 1000/1001 or WEST SYSTEM EPOXY to seal any voids or exposed fiberglass cloth. Then use thickened epoxy to fill and fair the crater. Do not use a soft, absorbent filler like microballoons or talc—absorption is what we are trying to prevent. Likewise, never use a soft cosmetic putty below the waterline. I use a two-component epoxy product like INTERLUX 417A/418B, WOOLSEY GOLD PRIMER, or PETTIT FLEXBOND MARINE EPOXY to produce a very fine surface finish. Try INTERLUX INTERPROTECT WATERTITE V135A/136A for a fast–drying, two-part epoxy for filling holes, scratches, and blisters. It has the consistency of butter, making it easy to smooth it out to a fine finish. Always sand the area after fillers have cured, to assure good adhesion of the next coat. Wash the hull thoroughly. Now all that remains is a barrier coat to seal the hull—and eliminate the original problem—and an antifouling paint.

applying a barrier coat, you will preserve or even enhance the value of most boats; by doing so while the bottom is clean, you'll save yourself the trouble of removing old bottom paint later. The exception may be with new boats. The gelcoat on a new boat may already deliver moisture resistance comparable to a barrier coat—there has been progress in the formulation of gelcoats—and sanding the gelcoat will probably void the warranty. Contact the manufacturer before barrier-coating a brand-new bottom.

Begin by scrubbing the bottom clean with a detergent, and rinsing thoroughly. Then proceed to the solvent wash recommended by the manufacturer of the barrier coat, which, in this description, is INTERLUX FIBERGLASS SOLVENT WASH 202. Completely wipe down the bottom with solvent wash, changing rags frequently. This step will remove any surface contamination or residual mold-release agent, and present a clean surface for the barrier coat (the mold–release agent is a silicone product applied to the boatbuilder's mold to allow easy separation of the finished hull from mold).

# Neil Wilson: Osmotic Blisters and Megayachts

After a 27-year career repairing boats, Neil Wilson now manages SouthBay Boat Yard in Chula Vista, California—five acres of vessels in every stage of construction and repair, within sight of the Mexican border. In addition to smaller pleasure boats, South-Bay Boat Yard also works on megayachts. In one corner of the yard sat a 22-foot Catalina sailboat, its underbelly pockmarked with thousands of blisters and marked notations of date and moisture content. Elsewhere, a 118-foot custom sailboat—complete with a mermaid tile mosaic in a shower enclosure—was in the final stages of construction. Wilson shared his thoughts about the local climate, linear polyurethane, and osmotic blisters:

## Climate

The Pacific Ocean off California is cold, at 55°F for much of the year. Slime and scum are rare in water this cold, although "coral" grows on bottoms on the southern coast. For antifouling we use **PRO LINE** paints at about the 60 percent cuprous level. **INTERLUX ULTRA-KOTE** and **PETTIT TRINIDAD** are also popular in this area. Out here, we can get three years from them. Some of our racing sailors put on four to five coats of ablative bottom paint, and burnish them down to a very fast surface.

Humidity is low, so mold and mildew that thrive in high humidity are rarely a problem. Offshore breezes sweep the air quite clean. In these conditions, a small recreational boat can go 10 years without serious cosmetic care. California boatowners avoid compounding with oxidation removers and instead generally rely on boat soaps and wax to protect the surfaces. After a cruise, a freshwater washdown with a soft brush and boat soap, followed by chamois, keeps a wax job acceptable for the better part of a year.

## Linear Polyurethane

The largest vessels we see go another route. Hauling, cleaning, and waxing a large vessel is a significant repetitive expense. The other option is to paint the topsides with linear polyurethane (also known as two-part polyurethane), which requires almost no care for many years. However, I would never paint a new small or mid-sized boat. Linear polyurethane is expensive and is best applied by professionals. Some say it can be done well by amateurs, but the risk of disappointment is high. To get a top-quality finish, you need a very handy person with the right equipment and the right conditions.

## Osmotic Blisters

There's only one way to deal with blisters: make sure you've gotten all of them. We never use chemical strippers—you're bound to miss a deep blister somewhere and in a couple of years it erupts. Here's what we do. After a power wash, we bring the boat into the sandblast shed where a professional with 20 years' experience sandblasts the hull, down to the fibers if necessary. Then, we power wash three times with a pressure of at least 3,000 pounds per square inch to remove every trace of loose residue, contaminants, uncured resin, and what have you. The result is a rough, clean surface that feels like cement, perfectly prepared for painting.

Then we leave the boat out in the sun. This is where the low humidity and hot sun of the Southwest come in. We check the moisture content of the fiberglass on a regular basis—hence the notations on the hull—until the hull has dried to below 4 percent moisture. Then we fill the craters with epoxy, using new fiberglass cloth to fill the deeper ones, fair the surface, apply four to five layers of barrier coat, and finally two coats of bottom paint. And that's a bottom we can guarantee for five years.

Spray some water on the bottom. If it beads up, you have not removed all the contaminants, and you should repeat the solvent wipe-down with INTERLUX FIBERGLASS SOLVENT WASH 202.

Rough up the gelcoat with 80-grit sandpaper. This step is critical to create "tooth" in the gelcoat. Remove the sanding dust with the same solvent wash. You'll notice that we always clean *before* sanding, to avoid embedding impurities in the surface, and we always use a solvent wash *after* sanding to remove any last impurities.

Apply four to five coats of INTERLUX INTERPROTECT 2000/2001 barrier coat, or WEST SYSTEM EPOXY with barrier additive, according to the manufacturer's instructions, to produce a dry-film thickness of 10 mils. Pay careful attention to the limits of time allowed between succeeding coats. Follow immediately with two coats of antifouling paint.

# Previously Painted Fiberglass Bottom

The bottom of the boat should be powerwashed immediately after the boat is taken out of the water. If the boat is not adequately powerwashed at haulout, the scum and slime will harden like cement. In that case, you may have to use a good hull cleaner. Try BOATLIFE FIBERGLASS POWDER CLEANER AND STAIN REMOVER and a scraper. If more is required, sand with a disk sander, or by hand, with 80-grit paper.

## Routine Recoating

Inspect the bottom. What you want to see is a smooth, clean surface with no sign of loose, flaking, or built-up paint—or more widespread adhesion problems. If the bottom is in good condition, and you know which antifouling paint is currently applied, bottom painting is straightforward. Lightly sand with 80-grit paper, wipe the bottom with the appropriate thinner, mask off the waterline with tape, and proceed with painting. Use the same antifouling paint as before, or one known to be compatible. If you are planning to change bottom paints, refer to the compatibility charts available from all bottom paint manufacturers, or call the manufacturer directly. If you don't know what paint was used previously, apply the new paint to a small area. After it dries completely, scratch at it with a putty knife. If it comes off easily, there is a compatibility problem. If a compatible antifouling paint cannot be found, the old bottom paint will have to be removed (see below).

The actual painting is easy. Stir the paint thoroughly to get the settled cuprous oxide off the bottom and mixed throughout. Use solvent-resistant rollers. Apply thick coatings. Don't skimp and try to roll out the paint to make it go further. Apply an extra coat of bottom paint on the keel, at the rudder and the waterline where water turbulence is greatest and paint wears more rapidly. Follow the time-to-launch instructions carefully, as uncured bottom paint will not adhere once it is in the water.

Take care not to cover sacrificial zincs with bottom paint, as they must be exposed to function. Likewise, transducers will not work if they are covered with bottom paint. If they get coated by mistake, clean them carefully with a soft brush. The new paint should come off easily. Raw-water intake strainers can be coated with antifouling paint but clear the openings with a screwdriver so water flow is not restricted. Plug through-hull fittings with rags while painting to keep them clear.

During the season, an occasional bottom scrub of a hard bottom paint will remove slime clogging the paint pores and expose the toxic, cuprous oxide to water so it may continue to do its job.

## Solvents and the Environment

Solvents used to clean and prepare surfaces for subsequent coatings are generally toxic and flammable. For example, most commercial paint strippers contain toxic methylene chloride. Though highly effective, this is a solvent of last resort. It must be removed within the time limit, as it may eat into the gelcoat. I prefer an environmentally safe marine paint stripper like PEEL AWAY MARINE SAFETY STRIP.

### Removing Old Bottom Paint

If the present paint has built up a thick deposit over the years, or if some widespread failure is taking place, or if the new paint is incompatible with the old, it is necessary to remove what remains and start from scratch. For an isolated patch, scrape off any loose chips with a hook scraper and sand down to the underlying gelcoat or barrier coat. The two standard methods of removing an entire coat of old bottom paint are chemical stripping, and scraping-and-sanding. Each of these methods requires you to capture the waste and dispose of it in a proper hazardous waste dumpsite.

PEEL AWAY MARINE SAFETY STRIP is an environmentally safe, yet expensive, paint stripper that contains no methylene chloride or other caustic agents normally found in hardware-store paint strippers. However, protective gloves and clothing should still be worn. The product will remove five or more layers of paint if applied up to ⅛ inch thick. The stripper is then covered with PEEL AWAY fibrous laminated cloth and left on for up to 48 hours. Waiting time usually takes two hours per coat of old paint before the stripper can be removed. The bottom paint is then stripped off by sliding a wide putty knife underneath the paint and easing the paint, paste, and cloth away in one piece. This mass of waste is then rolled up and disposed of responsibly. After rinsing and allowing the surface to dry, you may proceed to paint according to the new bottom paint's label directions.

Should you prefer the other method of removing bottom paint, scrape away all loose paint, then carefully sand down to the barrier coat or gelcoat. Wipe gelcoat with solvent to remove any mold-release agent exposed during sanding.

## Topsides

Before you paint the gelcoat topsides, stop and reconsider. Once you paint the gelcoat, you commit yourself to painting it forever. It is almost impossible to restore the original finish after painting. You should examine the gelcoat carefully to determine whether the surface is in fact recoverable with the use of rubbing compounds and gelcoat repair kits. (For more on gelcoat care, see chapter 2.)

There is always the temptation to try a less costly conventional paint from the hardware store, but remember the amount of time you squandered in preparation. Marine finishes are formulated to withstand extreme sun, moisture, and abrasion. It is a waste of effort to use a paint that is not formulated for the marine environment.

Consider the possibility of hiring a professional painter to apply a two-part linear polyurethane, versus your time and effort to learn how to apply linear polyurethane or a one-part urethane. Think about Neil Wilson's comments in his interview in this chapter.

## Types of Marine Topside Paints

When making your color choice, be aware that light topside colors will last longer than dark colors, because they reflect the sun's ultraviolet rays and do not absorb them, an activity that brings about eventual film destruction.

### TWO-PART POLYURETHANE

These coatings are often called linear polyurethanes or LPUs and are a blend of isocyanate, resins, ultraviolet absorbers, and modifying chemicals. A reaction takes place when the two parts are combined. It produces a very hard, high-gloss, and durable coating. The paint should be applied to a non-flexing surface where an extremely hard finish and exceptionally high gloss are called for, such as the topsides of a yacht. It can be applied with brush, roller, or spray. Spray-coating is preferably the domain of the professional. There is normally a long pot-life once the components are mixed, so there is no need to rush.

An advantage of linear polyurethanes over plain polyester gelcoat is that these finishes need almost no care for years. Conversely, maintaining unpainted gelcoat with cleaning, polishing, and the occasional use of oxidation removers is a frequent and time-consuming effort.

The two-part urethanes cure catalytically, and not only form a better, harder, and more brilliant coating than the one-component, modified, oil-based products but they typically cover in fewer coats and have noticeably better gloss and leveling characteristics. For the budget-minded, however, some compromise may be needed: a one-component urethane is easier to apply, and has initial gloss and longevity that is reasonable for a product costing 50 to 75 percent less. Linear urethanes are quite costly compared to other topside paints.

### ONE-PART POLYURETHANE

As a one-component paint, these coatings are normally urethane-modified, oil-based products that cure by the evaporation of a solvent. They have high resistance to abrasion and chemicals, giving them long life, high gloss, and color retention. They can be applied like any conventional paint. One-part urethanes are, however, not as durable as two-part urethanes.

## ALKYD-BASED ENAMELS

These conventional enamels are easy to apply and can give years of good results in less critical areas of the boat. Alkyd paints date back many years and are what we now refer to as "oil-based" paints. On land, they have been almost entirely replaced by water-based latex paints. For marine applications, alkyds still do a good job but are being replaced by one- and two-part urethanes. Normally, alkyds don't contain UV absorbers, and therefore don't last as long as polyurethanes.

## SPECIALTY FINISHES

These are generally alkyd-based paints that have silicone or Teflon added for improved resistance to staining. They are often easier to clean than conventional alkyds are.

## Topside Technique

If the surface is in good condition, it is probable that a cleaning followed by light sanding with 220-grit sandpaper will prepare the surface adequately for good topcoat adhesion. Wipe off any sanding residue with the appropriate solvent. If the surface is in poor condition, more aggressive cleaning and sanding will be required. Either spot-prime the repairs, or coat the entire surface with a recommended primer before applying the topcoat. Remember, any time epoxy has been used, the surface to be painted should be washed with water and detergent to remove amines, which will always blush to the surface. If not removed, these amines will prevent the paint film from adhering properly.

Apply two coats of topcoat, roughing up with 320- to 400-grit sandpaper between applications. Always paint in good weather. It is preferable to paint at least six hours before nightfall and the prospect of dew. Moisture on uncured paint can retard the cure and mottle the surface. Be careful not to abrade the paint surface for about a week until it becomes hard and is fully cured.

An amateur can achieve surprisingly good results with the roll-and-tip method: one person applies the paint with a roller, and a second person immediately follows behind, smoothing out the roller stipple with a long-bristled brush.

But first, remove loose fabric from the roller so you will not be putting hairs into the fresh film. Wad up some masking tape into a ball, and rub it on the roller. This will pick up all the loose hairs.

Roll the paint on vertically with a fairly dry roller in a four-foot-wide strip. The person with the brush should follow immediately behind. Holding the handle at approximately a 45-degree angle to the hull, wipe the brush horizontally, using only the tip. Immediately, finish tipping the same area in a vertical direction. This must be done quickly, as a thin coating of paint will begin to get tacky rapidly. The brusher should keep a plastic cup in the other hand to wipe excess paint off the brush tip.

# Doug Templin on Linear Polyurethanes

**Doug Templin** is the owner of DETCO Marine in Newport Beach, California, the West Coast distributor for Awlgrip and Sterling linear-polyurethane finishes, and the producer of its own line of adhesives and sealants. Given his expert knowledge of coatings and what makes them fail, he is often called as an expert witness at trials involving coating and laminate failure. His articles have appeared in *Professional Boatbuilder,* *WoodenBoat,* and *Sail* magazines.

"Linear-polyurethane finishes should no longer be thought of simply as paints," he said. "Most marine finishes are complex coating *systems*. Each step is an integral part of the success or failure of the end product. A full-blown system will probably encompass surface preparation, primers, fairing, barrier layers, and final coats.

"Once the surface has been prepared by stripping, sandblasting, or sanding, a primer layer should be applied. When the whole hull is being refinished, we apply a substrate primer as a foundation for all that follows. We usually use epoxy, which acts both as a primer for the topcoat and as a barrier coat for the hull (sealing out moisture). Whether you're using an epoxy or some other primer, read the instructions carefully to determine the time limits on subsequent coats. Some systems call for complete drying, followed by sanding and then recoating; others call for recoating while the primer is still 'green,' or uncured.

"Keep in mind that curing times speed up dramatically as the temperature increases. If you are supposed to recoat before the previous layer has fully cured, and you leave it too late, you will most likely have to sand before proceeding. To determine whether a coating has cured, simply rub the surface with the solvent required for the *next* layer. If the surface softens after a dozen or so rubs, it is still green. If not, it has cured. If the weather is cool, or if you are working under differing application techniques, amines in the hardener may percolate to the surface and, upon hitting the air, will form a greasy surface known as an 'amine blush.' If this blush is not removed, the next

Pour a half-hour's worth of paint into a disposable paint bucket and put the lid back on the can. Solvent loss will be minimized. Even though the paint looks unchanged, stir it occasionally to keep the pigments from settling out in the bottom of the can. There is no sense in painting with only the separated liquid component. Incidentally, it pays to wet the ground below the work area. If the wind kicks up, dust won't blow into your wet paint.

layer of coating will fail to adhere properly. You will have to wash the surface and sand before recoating. It's also a good idea to protect an epoxy primer coat from fog, rain, or dew, because epoxy is moisture-sensitive before it cures. If you're working outside, apply epoxy primer on a dry morning. Late-day applications invite failure caused by evening dew or night rains.

"Some users apply too many thin coats. They mistakenly believe that numerous wet-on-wet primer applications without sanding are better than a couple of thick coats with sanding in between. Follow the instructions for the system you are using. But keep in mind that the second approach is often preferable, as there is a greater chance of solvent retention in wet-on-wet applications. Any uncured ingredient trapped within the coating, whether it is an amine from the hardener or a slower-evaporating solvent, will find its way to the surface. If it is buried by the next layer of coating, the coats will not bond properly, and failure results. Press hard on the surface. If you can see your fingerprint or smell solvent on your fingers, you can bet there are solvents still present in the primer."

### Fairing and Painting

"The next step is to fair any scratches or gouges with putty. Most professional painters use solvent-free epoxy compounds for deep filling. In addition to their compatibility problems with epoxy primers, polyester and vinyl putties have serious drawbacks, ranging

from shrinkage and long cure times to slow solvent departure.

"The biggest problems we run into during painting are improper mixing and dust. Most multi-component paints require you to mix a resin, a hardener, and a thinner. Incomplete mixing or incorrect proportions are invitations to disaster. Once again, following the label directions is essential. Dust is another story. Most layers will require sanding, and it is crucial to remove dust before applying the next coat. Get rid of the dust with careful air blowing or a wipedown. Wash the surface with detergent, and rinse it well the night before.

"Immediately before painting, wipe the surface with the recommended solvent on a tack rag. Use lint-free rags like cloth diapers lightly saturated with the solvent. Don't use terry-cloth towels, as they hold too much solvent. Wipe it on quickly, then off with a clean rag. Dust can also be a problem if you apply too many light coats: they will inevitably catch more dust. A couple of coats of the proper thickness will minimize dust collection. Apply enough paint in the first coat to get good coverage and an even surface. If dust does land on the final coat, most professionals will sand and redo the whole coat rather than sand the problem area and buff with compound. Buffing will show as a spot if done even on a small area, and will lose its luster before the rest of the boat. Buffing out a few bug tracks or sags with 1,500- or 2,000-grit paper, or a fine rubbing compound, is fine, but not on anything larger than that."

## Accent Paints and Graphics

Most marine-coating manufacturers produce small cans of striping enamel. Applied over a solvent-cleaned surface, they will give a durable, high-gloss finish. They will hide the substrate easily and are simple to apply. Choose striping masking tape carefully. 3M produces a series of tapes specially formulated for creating a sharp edge for applying striping paint. 3M #256/SCOTCH GREEN MASKING TAPE and 3M #471 SCOTCHVINYL TAPE are

## Cleaning Paintbrushes

Paintbrushes can be extremely difficult to clean. If you plan to use one again soon, try rinsing the brush with thinner and shaking it dry in a paper bag. This is a laughable sight, but it works. If it will be a while before you want to use it again, clean the brush with solvent, then wash it thoroughly in detergent and water, rinse, comb out the bristles, and store it wrapped in newspaper. Another technique is to rinse the brush in kerosene, then dip it in engine oil and wrap it in plastic. Rinse the brush in kerosene before using it again.

recommended by 3M as the boot-striping tapes to use. **3M #256** can be left on the boat up to five days and **3M #471** can be left on for up to a month.

Don't make the mistake of leaving masking tape on longer than recommended. When the adhesive is exposed to sunlight, it becomes almost impossible to remove. Use **3M General Purpose Adhesive Cleaner** or **Goo Gone** to clean off any adhesive residue left after the masking tape is removed. Apply a polymer polish like **Star brite Premium Marine Polish with Teflon** to the accent and boot stripes.

Plastic graphics are easy to apply, but first dewax the area with acetone. Tape the plastic lettering to the hull once it is in proper alignment. Make small marks at the corners to aid in placing the graphics. Next, remove the lettering and peel off the backing. Professionals spray the back side of the graphic or letters with water containing a few drops of detergent. This allows the plastic to be slid into its precise location. Press the lettering tape against the hull and smooth out any bubbles with the side of your hand. Smooth out the tape with a squeegee. Prick any large air bubbles with a pin and smooth the letters out again. Use the same polymer polish on the letters as was used on the rest of the topsides. You'll be surprised at how inexpensive and easy the job is, and how professional the outcome.

## Deck

Most deck coatings are the same as those used on the sides of the boat. The main difference is that decks cannot have a high gloss as they will be slippery. Much of the walking area on newer boats has a nonskid surface that consists of gelcoat with a pattern molded into the surface. It is almost impossible to sand or even thoroughly clean deep down into these patterns. However, if the skid-proof deck ages to the point where it must be painted, proceed as follows. Using bronze wool and a solvent wash, scrub the skid-proof surface thoroughly. Apply a thin primer like **Interlux AL 200 Fiberglass Primer** or **Pettit 6999.** Apply a good topside or deck coating. Polymeric beads can be added to the paint if the nonskid surface needs to be made rougher. Consider using **Interlux Polymeric Noskid Compound 2398** or **Woolsey Non-Skid Compound.**

## Wood

Many different woods are used on boats, but all share the same characteristics. All wood absorbs moisture and is considered flexible. Unprotected wood is susceptible to drying, swelling, rot, and all manner of accidental contaminants. With the exception of teak, wood used on boats needs to be protected by a flexible finish that is impervious to water. Although this is not difficult to achieve, wood is harder to protect than fiberglass is. Wood found on a fiberglass boat will often be decorative, and varnish is commonly used to protect and enhance it.

In general, new bare wood should be coated as soon as possible. If wood is allowed to absorb moisture, it may undermine subsequent painting or varnishing. A bare wood surface that has aged and grayed must be prepared for coating by sanding, or by using a wood cleaner and bleach. To prepare for painting, sand with 80-grit sandpaper; for varnishing, use 150- to 180-grit sandpaper. Remove sanding dust with the recommended thinner. Prime, using the paint or varnish diluted 10 to 20 percent with the thinner recommended for the topcoat. Diluted, the coating will sink into the wood, giving a good grip for subsequent coats. Follow the specific dilution instructions on the can. Any paint suitable for topsides application may be used on wood. Apply the coating as directed. When instructed, sand between coats to ensure good inter-coat adhesion and a smooth final finish.

## Sandpaper Sequence

Gradually going from coarse sandpaper to fine sandpaper will produce a perfect surface for painting. Many people neglect to sand the primer, thinking that the finish coat will cover all imperfections. Sand the primer, too. You will not be able to see the scratches left by 220-grit paper, but they are there, and the finish coat of paint will expose them. A final sanding polish with 320-grit paper will remove these scratches.

The sandpaper sequences are

- Primer-coat grits: 80, 120, 220, and 320
- Finish-coat grits: 180, 220, 320, and 400

## Keeping Sandpaper Dry

Keep sandpaper from picking up the moisture that is almost always present on the boat by storing it in a sealed ZIPLOC bag.

Teak is the exception to the coating rule. Many boaters don't coat teak; instead, they leave it to the elements. Teak is a very weather-resistant wood and will turn a pleasant light gray if left alone. Since you are probably washing the boat down after every trip, make a little additional effort and wash the untreated teak deck with salt water, not potable water. The salt will act as a bleach and keep mildew from growing on the edges. For more on teak and teak-treatment options, see page 79.

## Painting

In most cases, painting wood means recoating previously painted surfaces. Routine touch-ups will make a sound painted surface last for many years. If painted surfaces are not kept clean or touched up, they will deteriorate to the point where they must be stripped and removed. (Stripping wood is covered in the Varnishing section below.) Check the condition of the existing surface before moving ahead.

If the surface is in good condition, a cleaning followed by a light sanding with 200-grit sandpaper should prepare the surface adequately for a refresher coat, and provide good topcoat adhesion. Wipe off any sanding residue with an appropriate solvent.

Between coats, it's standard practice to use 320- to 400-grit sand-paper, but defer to the instructions on the can. If the surface is in poor condition, more aggressive cleaning and sanding will be required. Remember to wipe the dust off with solvent rags. Either spot-prime or coat the entire surface with a primer before applying the topcoat. Apply two coats of topcoat, using 320- to 400-grit sandpaper between coats.

## Varnishing

Paint may seal and protect the boat's woodwork perfectly, but it will never quicken the boater's pulse like the sight of a fine wood grain glowing through a varnish. In essence, a varnish is a coating without pigment. EPI-FANES GLOSS VARNISH or PETTIT EASYPOXY HIGH-BUILD are traditional tung-oil-based varnishes that have above-average gloss retention and hold up quite well to weather.

Another whole category of varnishes is made with one-part poly-urethane and is the subject of much debate. Supporters say they offer a harder, more durable surface; critics say they are prone to early adhesion failure. In any case, remember, all varnishes suffer from the ravages of sun and salt, particularly in tropical climates. Varnishes deteriorate faster in the elements than does paint, which is loaded with pigments to reflect the sun's rays. Varnish manufacturers are now including ultraviolet absorbers in their formulations to delay destruction of the varnish from sunlight. Even so, varnish should get a refresher coat every few months.

### PREPARING WOOD

The rationale for going to all the trouble of varnishing is to produce a deep, rich, golden finish so the beauty of the wood can be clearly seen, a distinct image that speaks of excellence. Preparing wood for a coating of varnish is hard work but immensely satisfying. If the wood is varnished, or coated with a hybrid like SIKKENS CETOL (see page 79), there are a number of ways to strip off the old finish: a heat gun, a chemical stripper, acid bleach, dry scraping, or sanding. If it is new, bare wood, all that is required is a light sanding. If it's oiled or weathered wood, you must sand and wash with solvent. You have to be a fanatic to enjoy this job, but think ahead to that day when you can sit back and enjoy the compliments.

Professionals use a heat gun to remove old varnish, then follow with a chemical stripper to get what remains of the coating that burrowed deep down in the wood pores. To do a good job, you'll need a heat gun, a pull-type scraper, and a fine file to sharpen the scraper. It helps to round the edges of the scraper to prevent gouging. A vacuum cleaner, used frequently, captures the incredible amount of debris that otherwise would drift into every corner and crevice of the boat.

Varnish can be removed with triangular scrapers bought at a hardware store. Broken pieces of windowpane also make great scrapers. Place a piece of glass between two sheets of newspaper and rap it with a hammer.

Select pieces that have the exact round edge or sharp point to fit into the odd-shaped angles or grooves of your project. The sharp glass edge dulls about as fast as a metal scraper will. Wear gloves and be careful as you hold the piece. With broken glass, it's possible to produce a scraped surface as smooth as one that 220-grit sandpaper can provide.

When you're using a heat gun, aim the nozzle at a 45-degree angle to the surface, keeping it about an inch away, until the old varnish bubbles. Flip the heat gun up in the air to divert the heat temporarily, and immediately scrape toward you. A common tendency is to want to scrape away, following closely behind the bubbling varnish, but there is less chance of gouging the wood if you pull the scraper toward you.

Don't blast a heat gun's high temperatures onto adjacent gelcoat. Cover any fiberglass near the area to be stripped with **3M #2070 SAFE RELEASE MASKING TAPE**, a protective tape that has a low-tack adhesive and produces a sharp edge for easy removal from freshly painted surfaces. If you're using a heat gun, cover the first tape with normal masking tape. If you're using a chemical stripper, cover the first tape with **3M #226 SOLVENT RESISTANT MASKING TAPE**. This black tape resists all conventional solvents and, if necessary, withstands weather for up to three months.

Gently apply the paint remover along the wood grain. Bronze wool or terry-cloth towels rubbed on the wood will remove the softened paint. When you've finished, always remove the masking tape by pulling the tape back on itself. Put the sticky mess in a paper shopping bag to get it out of the way.

When you've gone as far as you can with the heat gun, move on to the next step, chemical stripping. Wear a mask and chemical-resistant gloves. Chemical strippers soften the varnish by saturating the coating with solvents. Use **3M #2070 SAFE RELEASE MASKING TAPE** to protect any nearby fiberglass or paint from being damaged by the stripper. Put a sacrificial layer of conventional masking tape on top of the **3M #2070 TAPE**. Remove both tapes as soon as the surface has been cleaned.

If practical, remove the wood parts you want to strip and varnish. Put them in a tray or bucket, and spread copious amounts of chemical stripper on the wood. Cover it with plastic wrap for a minimum of 15 minutes. Re-apply the stripper if you see any areas that have dried out. Scrub with a nylon brush and lacquer thinner to remove the stripper. Repeat, applying lacquer thinner until all the chemical stripper and varnish are removed. Wipe the wood with a cloth soaked in lacquer thinner. If some varnish remains in the wood grooves, scrub the spot carefully with a nylon toothbrush.

Often, you'll find it's too much work to remove wood parts because of all the screws that need to be removed and then re-bedded. If this is

## Varnish Like a Pro

If you want the best-looking boat in the marina, I recommend you find a copy of *Brightwork: The Art of Finishing Wood* (International Marine), by Rebecca Wittman. It is the best all-around treatise on finishing wood. She will make you work hard for mirror-like brightwork, but it is worth every sore muscle to see the results.

Wood

the case, coat any nearby metal parts with petroleum jelly. Varnish will not adhere to the greasy surface and the mess wipes off the metal easily when the job is finished.

### APPLYING VARNISH

Always clean the varnish brush in the recommended solvent before beginning. Cleaning will rid the brush of any contaminants picked up while it was stored in the locker.

If you use varnish straight from the can, there's a strong probability that foreign matter will get into the can and spoil the perfect surface you're trying to create. Pour a reasonable amount of varnish into a separate container. Always use a clean brush.

It's almost impossible to do a good job of varnishing inside the cabin unless there is good light on the wood. Rig up whatever light is possible, so you can watch out for voids, runs, and areas not uniformly brushed out. Don't just check the varnish by looking straight down at the wet surface. Bend over and look *across* the work from an acute angle. You'll see every little imperfection.

Add at least 15 to 20 percent of the appropriate thinner to varnish for the first coat on bare wood. It will penetrate into the wood fibers and prime the subsequent layers of varnish. Reduce the proportion of thinner as you proceed and leave the final coats unthinned. Sand lightly between coats to remove blemishes and roughen the surface for the next coat. I usually apply between five and eight coats before achieving the final finish I want.

Clean the brush, using the recommended thinners. One of the best ways to keep a clean varnish brush in good shape for the next job is to clean it in thinner, then wash it in detergent and water. Rinse it thoroughly. Dry the brush and wrap it tightly in a brown paper bag. Hang it by the handle so the brush keeps its shape. Clean it in the recommended thinner before using it again.

Wet splatters can be removed, before they dry, with the varnish thinner. If you find some old splatters that you missed in cleaning up after varnishing, try first to carefully pop the spots off with the corner of a razor blade. If you can't remove it, dab a little INTERLUX PINTOFF 299E or BOATLIFE FIBERGLASS BOTTOM PAINT REMOVER on the spot with a toothpick. Let it sit for a few minutes, then wipe it off. Clean the area with lacquer thinner and re-wax.

### MAINTAINING VARNISH

To touch up scratched or gouged areas, first clean the damaged area with the solvent recommended on the varnish can. Lightly sand with 320-grit paper so there is no ridge line on the scratch. Clean the area a second time with the same solvent. Tape off any nearby metal or fiberglass, then varnish the spot with enough coats to match the surrounding area.

To keep the varnish you worked on so hard looking like new, apply a refresher every few months. To prepare the surface for a refresher coat, clean any grime off the varnish with MURPHY'S OIL SOAP and rinse. Wipe with alcohol and water. Sand softly with 320-grit paper. Wipe down with the recommended solvent. Apply two light coats of varnish with a minimum of 24 hours between coats. The varnish should be completely removed when the surface integrity is broken and strips of varnish begin to sheet off.

## A Stand-Out Teak Treatment

There are dozens of products, even more theories, and little agreement on how to treat exterior teak. Traditionalists will varnish. Others will oil. Those too busy with other projects will leave their teak to nature and let it turn gray like the shingles of a Nantucket cottage. But there is a middle ground. In my experience, the easiest and longest-lasting way to treat teak and other exterior woods is to apply multiple coats of SIKKENS CETOL marine finish, a translucent, breathable, protective finish for application over clean wood. It is easy to apply and has an excellent track record for longevity. The Sikkens company suggests that you not sand between coats because sanding will remove too much of the protective coating. I have found that the final surface texture can be improved if, between coats, you wipe the surface down briskly with a terry-cloth towel. It will knock off those little bumps that mysteriously appear from an occasional bubble or trapped dust. If you feel that some CETOL has been removed by this rubbing, apply a fourth coat to give additional protection.

When your CETOL finish shows yellow streaks, you will have to sand down to bare wood before recoating. If it has merely dulled, touch up now. Unlike varnish, CETOL can be touched up easily. But before you apply a touch-up to a scratch in the surface, be sure to clean the area by scrubbing vigorously across the grain with a nylon pad and detergent. Rinse and dry thoroughly. Within a week of cleaning, apply a liberal coating of CETOL using a bristle brush. Use regular varnish brushes, as foam pads splatter this thin solution too easily.

## Specialized Masking Tapes

3M makes 12 masking tapes for marine use. Each has a specific application. Knowing which tape to use can make a world of difference to the final results and the post-project clean-up. Try to select a tape that closely fits your requirements. Pay attention to how long the tape will stay on the boat, how much it must curve, how much solvent resistance is required, how weather-resistant it must be, and whether you need extremely fine-line separation. There are other brands available, but I don't know of another manufacturer who covers the waterfront as well as 3M.

If masking tape is not removed from fiberglass or wood surfaces within the time limits indicated by the manufacturer, the adhesive will come off the tape and adhere tenaciously to the surface. It is difficult to remove the adhesive with conventional cleaners. GOO GONE and 3M GENERAL PURPOSE ADHESIVE CLEANER are products specifically manufactured to remove adhesives and should work in most cases.

Wood

## The Best Gloss in the Marina

Outside the boating industry, there are hobbyists and sporting equipment manufacturers who create a gloss on wood that is unsurpassed. Properly applied, a good marine varnish can be applied to make a finish equivalent to that on wooden golf clubs. Think of their gloss; the depth of sheen and image. Golf-club manufacturers use a soft muslin wheel and a German buffing compound called **GLADZ WOCH** to bring out an almost perfect shine. If you want your wood to shine like nothing you've ever seen before,

call the plating sources in the Yellow Pages. Hopefully, you will locate a local supplier of **GLADZ WOCH**. There may be an area on the boat, such as the instrument panel, that would be worth the effort. Similarly, ornamental knife manufacturers produce wooden knife handles with an almost impossibly perfect sheen by using a product called **MICROMESH**. It's manufactured by Micro Surface Finish Products, Box 818, Wilton, IA 52778.

# *Quick-Reference Guide*

## Selection and Application of Coatings

| | TOPIC | JOB | PAGE | PRODUCT | HOW TO DO JOB |
|---|---|---|---|---|---|
| **Below waterline** | Aluminum | Bottom painting | 65 | INTERLUX PRIMEWASH VINY-LUX 353/354; PETTIT METAL PRIMER | Clean with solvent wash. Sandblast or use emery cloth. Prime with **353/354**. Apply 2 coats aluminum antifouling paint. |
| | Outboards and inboard-outboards | Painting lower unit | 65 | INTERLUX VINY-LUX PRIMEWASH 353/354; INTERLUX TRI-LUX II AEROSOL KIT; INTERLUX UNDERWATER PRIMER 360 | Clean unit thoroughly. Sand old paint with 80 grit. Prime with INTERLUX VINY-LUX PRIMEWASH **353/354**. Apply two coats TRI-LUX aerosol or brush on UNDERWATER PRIMER **360**. Apply multiple coats of aluminum antifouling paint. |
| | Bare fiberglass bottoms | Bottom painting | 66, 68 | INTERLUX FIBERGLASS SOLVENT WASH 202; INTERLUX INTERPROTECT 2000/2001; WEST SYSTEM EPOXY BARRIER ADDITIVE; bottom paint | Power wash. Wipe down with SOLVENT WASH **202**. Rough-sand with 80 grit. Solvent wash. Apply 10 mils of **2000/2001** or WEST SYSTEM. Water-wash hull. Apply 2 coats bottom paint. |
| | Previously painted bottoms | Bottom painting | 68 | INTERLUX FIBERGLASS SOLVENT WASH 202; INTERLUX INTERPROTECT 1000/1001; WEST SYSTEM EPOXY; bottom paint | Power wash. Wipe down with SOLVENT WASH **202**. Spot prime with **1000/1001**. Fairing compound in repair areas. Water-wash hull. Sand with 80 grit. Solvent wash. 2 coats bottom paint. |
| | | Repairing osmotic blisters | 66 | INTERLUX INTERPROTECT 1000/1001; INTERLUX 417A/418B; WOOLSEY GOLD PRIMER; INTERLUX INTERPROTECT WATERTITE V135A/136A; INTERLUX INTERPROTECT 2000/2001 | Open blisters and allow to dry. Wipe with SOLVENT WASH **202**. Apply **1000/1001** to any exposed fibers. Apply WATERTITE V135 to to fill holes. Water-wash hull. Sand. Solvent wash. Apply 10 mils of **2000/2001**. Water-wash hull. Apply 2 bottom coats. |

*continues*

# Quick-Reference Guide

## Selection and Application of Coatings (cont.)

| TOPIC | JOB | PAGE | PRODUCT | HOW TO DO JOB |
|---|---|---|---|---|
| | Removing bottom paint | 69 | PEEL AWAY MARINE SAFETY STRIP | Power-wash. Apply PEEL AWAY. Cover with PEEL AWAY cloth. Strip off cover, stripper, and bottom paint. |
| **Above waterline** | Topside painting | 71 | INTERLUX AL 200 FIBERGLASS PRIMER; INTERLUX BRIGHTSIDE | Clean. Light sand with 220-grit paper. Spot prime or coat all with primer. Apply 2 coats of paint. Roughen up with 320- or 400-grit paper between coats. |
| | Accent and boot stripes | Masking | 73–74 | 3M 256 SCOTCH/GREEN MASKING TAPE; 3M 471 SCOTCH VINYL TAPE; GOO GONE; 3M GENERAL PURPOSE ADHESIVE CLEANER | Clean surface with solvent wash. Mask with appropriate tape. Remove tape as soon as possible after painting. GOO GONE or 3M GENERAL PURPOSE ADHESIVE CLEANER will remove any adhesive residue. |
| | Deck | Painting | 74 | INTERLUX AL 200 FIBERGLASS PRIMER; PETTIT 6999; INTERLUX POLYMERIC NOSKID COMPOUND 2398 | Clean deck. Apply AL 200. Apply good topside or deck coating. Add polymeric beads to paint for nonskid. |
| | Painted wood surface | Painting | 75 | Solvent wash | Clean. Sand with 220-grit paper. Solvent clean. Apply 2 topcoats. |
| | Unpainted wood | Coating | 75 | Wood bleach; varnish or paint | Sand or bleach bare wood. 80-grit sand surface. Prime with 15-percent-reduced paint or varnish. Apply paint or varnish as directed on label. |
| | Stripping paint or varnish | Preparing surface for coating | 77 | 3M #2070 SAFE RELEASE MASKING TAPE; 3M #226 SOLVENT RESISTANT MASKING TAPE | Apply #2070 covered with #226 on areas needing protection. Apply stripper. Rub off with toweling. |

| TOPIC | JOB | PAGE | PRODUCT | HOW TO DO JOB |
|---|---|---|---|---|
| Varnishing | Stripping | 77 | Nylon brush; lacquer thinner | Remove part. Spread chemical stripper on parts in bucket. Clean off with lacquer thinner. |
| | Protection of nearby parts | 78 | Petroleum jelly | Protect nearby parts from stripper by coating with petroleum jelly. |
| | Varnishing | 78 | **EPIFANES GLOSS VARNISH; PETTIT EASYPOXY HIGH-BUILD** | Thin first coat 15 to 20 percent to prime bare wood. Follow with 5 to 7 coats. |
| | Cleaning splatters | 78 | **INTERLUX PINTOFF 299E; BOATLIFE FIBERGLASS BOTTOM PAINT REMOVER** | First try to pop splatters off with a razor blade. Soften with **PINTOFF 299E.** |
| Refresher coating | Varnishing | 79 | **MURPHY'S OIL SOAP** | Clean with **MURPHY'S OIL SOAP**. Rinse. Wipe with alcohol and water. Soft-sand with 320-grit. Wipe with solvent. Apply 2 coats varnish. |
| Teak finishing | Coating | 79 | **SIKKENS CETOL MARINE FINISH** | Clean surface. Sand. Solvent wash. Apply 3 coats of **CETOL** with no sanding between coats. |
| | Touch-ups | 79 | **SIKKENS CETOL MARINE FINISH** | Clean surface with nylon pad and detergent. Solvent wipe. Apply **CETOL**. |

# SEALANTS AND ADHESIVES

In this chapter, we will discuss the ways that sealants and adhesives work, different types of systems (and the resins that make them differ), some preferred products and applications, and finally, products for specific surfaces.

## What Are Sealants and Adhesives?

In the simplest terms, a sealant is a compound whose purpose is to seal out moisture, air, or contaminants, and to protect a surface from ultraviolet rays. It *seals* or isolates the area it covers. 3M POLYSULFIDE MARINE SEALANT 101, when used to bed deck hardware, is an example of a sealant.

An adhesive bonds two or more surfaces. PASCO-FIX Super Glue is an example of an adhesive for quickly gluing two nonporous surfaces. With many marine products, the line between sealant and adhesive cannot be drawn sharply. Some products are used as both sealants and adhesives. For the purpose of this chapter, I'll often combine the two as one, a sealant-adhesive.

The two most important characteristics of sealants and adhesives are durability and elasticity. Anything bonded or sealed must last for years, yet be elastic enough to withstand constant flexing. Most applications, such as bedding for a winch or a cleat, should use a sealant with sufficient flexibility to withstand exceptional shock-loads. In a few cases, an adhesive sealant must accept a structural load, and will therefore be less flexible. In every case, however, the bond must retain its intended characteristic for a long time, hopefully for the life of the boat.

This, however, is wishful thinking. As all of us know, there's a never-ending list of deck parts that need to be replaced and subsequently re-bonded. There are repairs to be made to the gelcoat. There are ports to rebed, headliners to reattach, rotten wood to replace. The list could be endless.

# Clearing up the Confusion

What could be better for a chapter on sealants and adhesives than talking to someone who restores old boats, making them look like they just came out of the dealer's showroom? **Mike Kennedy** is one of the rare breed of boatowners who are willing to prepare a

wood surface by using five ascending grades of sandpaper before the first drop of varnish touches his wood. He is the type of perfectionist who has tried every adhesive or sealant he could find in his never-ending search for the best product.

Mike has spent his adult life restoring old Chris-Crafts to look better than new. His boats have won numerous awards, yet the real satisfaction comes from his own pleasure in bringing back to life a timeless classic.

Mike started restoring Chris-Craft boats in the 1960s, and his present masterpiece is a 40-foot, 1953 Express Cruiser. In his spare time, Mike was marketing manager for M&E Marine.

I asked Mike to clear up the confusion regarding sealants and adhesives. What is the deciding factor in choosing one type of sealant instead of another?

"There are four kinds of sealants and adhesives produced for boats: polyurethanes, polysulfides, hybrids, and silicones. Let's take them one at a time," he said.

"The most popular polyurethane is **3M 5200**. This is the only product that is truly an adhesive and a sealant. It should only be used when adhesion is required, like at the hull-and-deck joint, or anything struc-

Sealants and adhesives are in many ways similar to coatings. They, too, are composed of resins, pigments, and additives. Unthickened epoxy or polyester resin systems have no pigment, and are similar in composition to varnishes. They are applied as a coating would be, with the consistency of honey.

Many sealants are called putties, caulks, or bedding compounds. They're made of resin and additives, and extended with pigments and fillers to make them viscous, so they'll adhere to vertical surfaces, fill deep holes, and match the color of the surrounding material. They are generally applied with a putty knife or caulking gun, or squeezed out of a tube.

They are similar to coatings in another way, too. Sealants-adhesives are sold both as one-component systems (like putties), or as two separate components that you must mix before application. An example of a one-

tural. It should never be used if there is the slightest possibility of having to replace the part. Though most people know this, 5200 is often misused. Another limitation to 5200 is that it does not stand up well to sunshine, and it should be painted if it's exposed to the elements. **3M 4200** is a polyurethane that is formulated to have poorer adhesion properties, allowing parts bedded with it to be removed.

"The second category is polysulfides. **BOAT-LIFE LIFE CALK** polysulfide is made of one-part Thiokol rubber. When it's used above the waterline, to bed deck fittings, rails, or cleats, it is the product of choice. It is often used below the waterline for through-hulls and struts, as a couple of examples. Polysulfides do not adhere as well as polyurethane and are therefore quite easily removed. They should be used to bed parts that will some day be replaced.

"Third, there are the hybrid sealants. **BOAT-LIFE LIFE SEAL** is a polyurethane-and-silicone combination that has approximately the same adhesive strength as polysulfide. It is the best product for bedding windows. One of the things I like about it is that it gives a nice glossy finish when it dries.

"And last, silicone. I may be off base here, but I don't think silicones belong on a boat. In a home ap-

plication they are fine, but the salt and dampness on a boat cause them to fail more often than not. Silicone has poor adhesive properties and will break up in time. The only place I would use a straight silicone on my boat is on Lexan."

I asked Mike if there was a good waterproof glue.

"Resorcinol is talked about all the time. It's the glue used in outdoor plywood. It would be worth a try. I use **WEST SYSTEM EPOXY**. It works as well as anything I've found.

"I even use epoxy to repair minor wood rot. If the rot is severe, I don't try to repair it. I replace it. **GIT-ROT** is a popular wood-rot reconstruction epoxy, but you can use **WEST SYSTEM EPOXY** just as well. The secret is to thin it with temperature. Leave parts A and B in the hot sun before you mix them. The sun will warm the two parts and thin them from their honey-like flow to an almost water-like, pourable consistency perfectly suited for seeping into the open pores of rotted wood.

"Sealants and adhesives are no mystery. Read labels and ask your friends at the marina or marine store. Everyone will have a story to tell about a sealant or adhesive project and give you some ideas."

component product is, again, **3M 101**. Examples of two-component systems are epoxies or polyesters. Generally, the two-component systems are more difficult to work with, but end up with superior strength and durability.

Here are some of the characteristics you should consider when deciding what type of product to choose:

- What is the purpose?
- Will it be used above the waterline, or below?
- Must the end result be flexible, or are you seeking a strong, rigid bond?
- Durability? Is the application meant to be permanent, or will you possibly replace it at some future date?

➤ How much time can you give it cure? (Launching time can be decisive in choosing a slow-curing or fast-curing product.)

➤ What conditions will the bond be exposed to? Salt water? Freezing temperatures? Flexing?

➤ Do you want to sand it easily after it's cured?

➤ Should the product be easy to clean from around the work area, and from your tools?

➤ Is cost a consideration?

# Before You Start

Before beginning any project involving sealants or adhesives, you should ask yourself some questions. Your choice of product will often depend on the answers to the following questions or the results of the following actions.

### WHAT EXACTLY DO YOU NEED TO DO?

Should the part be removed and replaced? Should only the fasteners be re-placed? Should the piece be reinforced with a backing plate now that you have everything apart? Is the time required for a completed cure a factor?

### PREPARE THE SURFACE

Once you have decided what to do, carefully remove the part and prepare the surface. Old parts bedded with silicone or polysulfide sealants (see below) will be relatively easy to remove with a putty knife. Parts glued with a polyurethane sealant will require extra effort, as a putty knife or solvent will not release the part. The use of excessive force will almost certainly damage the substrate, however, so work *carefully* on the sealant seam with a curved linoleum knife. Peel away the sealant as you pry the part up gently. If all else fails, warm the part with a heat gun. That may soften the sealant enough to loosen its bond to the substrate. Be careful not to let the hot air damage the part or the nearby substrate.

Once you have the part off, remove any contaminants and old sealant. Roughen up the surface, if necessary. Clean it well with a solvent wash of acetone or lacquer thinner. A clean surface is essential for almost any sealant or adhesive to live up to its potential.

### WHAT PRODUCT DO YOU NEED?

Decide what's needed to give the right amount of adhesion and protection to the part. For example, does it need a very flexible sealant? Is the surface open and porous, like wood, or nonporous, like metal? Should a better ad-hesive be chosen than was used last time, to make the joint more moisture-resistant and to prevent a recurrence of the present problem? Will the part ever need to be replaced again in the lifetime of the boat? Is cost a factor?

How much time do you have for the project? Can you do the job yourself or should a professional be brought in?

### READ THE LABELS

Look at the labels to find out what the main ingredient is. Unlike paints, sealants and adhesives don't always make their components obvious. They rely more on brand-name popularity. Read the label to establish what the main resin is, and refer to the information on resin performance given later in this chapter. It will help you choose the correct product.

### SELECT THE PRODUCT

Now that you know what is required, select the right product for the sealant or adhesive job. It is surprisingly simple when you know what each product's strong points and weaknesses are. Choose the correct product from the usage descriptions in this chapter.

### APPLY THE PRODUCT

Carefully read the chosen product's label for safety and application instructions. Many sealant and adhesive products have highly toxic components, so don't take the label instructions lightly. Follow them to the letter. Application instructions are given because manufacturers have found, through the years, that there are ways to make their products work best. If you follow their instructions, you'll almost always get a satisfactory result. But don't expect miracles if you just squeeze the product onto some broken, dirty surface on a cold, rainy afternoon. It won't do the job. Incidentally, be sure to wash your hands immediately after using any adhesive.

### CLEAN UP

Removing excess sealant or adhesive is obviously easiest before the product has cured. Once they've cured, many products will be difficult to remove. Read the label instructions on the sealant or adhesive for the recommended procedure for removing uncured and cured excess product. If you're in doubt, carefully use either acetone or 3M GENERAL PURPOSE ADHESIVE CLEANER. You'd be wise to wear rubber gloves when applying these solvents.

## Types of Sealant-Adhesives

There are as many categories of sealant-adhesives as there are types of coatings. Every year, new products or combinations of products come on the market touting their solutions to marine problems. However, there are a dozen proven generic categories of products that have their special boat uses. Many can be used for almost all applications, but are best for only a few. To choose the best, think carefully of what you want to accomplish, what you need to prevent from happening again, and what your own capabilities are.

## Two-Component Systems

As a rule, two-component systems are stronger than one-component systems. They are also more expensive, have a shorter pot life, and are harder to work with.

These systems normally cure by exothermic reaction: as the mixture reacts, heat is released. If you try to mix too large a batch, heat builds up rapidly and cannot escape, causing the mix to cure prematurely. A greater number of smaller batches allows you to work at a less frantic pace. Examples of two-component systems are resin/hardener mixes in epoxies, polyesters, and vinylesters.

### EPOXIES

WEST SYSTEM and EVERCOAT epoxy reaction-cure systems are composed of two parts, a resin and a hardener. They are effective above and below the waterline. Epoxy has superior adhesion, hardness, durability, and strength; it also absorbs less water than polyester does. But it is consistently more expensive. Epoxy can be used on most clean surfaces but should be the product of choice when you want a very strong bond between two non-porous surfaces.

Epoxy comes in many forms. Depending on the manufacturer and the use, either component can be purchased as a paste or a liquid. Pastes are often better for filling holes, or for vertical surfaces. It's easy to add a filler to thicken the epoxy, so that it has the consistency of a free-flowing honey or peanut butter. Once you mix the two components, the system begins to react and harden. Follow the label directions for the timing between coats. Choose your epoxy carefully: epoxies with a one-to-one mix ratio will not be as strong as those with a one-to-five or a one-to-seven ratio. Don't increase the amount of hardener to speed up the cure rate. You can do this with polyesters, but it's not advised with epoxies.

When the surface is meticulously clean, epoxy will adhere to almost anything. But, as accommodating as they are, epoxies will not grip well to polypropylene and polyethylene. This convenient characteristic allows epoxy to be mixed, pumped, and squeegeed using containers and tools made of these plastics.

If you're using regular hardener, your epoxy will be tack-free in 10 to 30 minutes, and cured solid in 6 to 15 hours, depending on the temperature, additives, and other variables.

The all-round best and most comprehensive booklet on epoxy repairs and construction is the *West System Fiberglass Boat Repair and Maintenance* booklet. You'll find it at most marine stores for about $3. Don't attempt a major project without referring to this easy-to-read treatise. There is a similar booklet on wood repairs called *West System Wood Repair and Maintenance.*

### POLYESTER

Polyester resins, combined with fiberglass matting and cloth, are the basic materials used in the construction of almost all fiberglass boats. EVERCOAT

POLYESTER LAMINATING RESIN is a two-component, reaction-cure system of resin and hardener that is most effective for above-the-waterline repairs. Below the waterline, polyester gelcoat is not waterproof, which leads to the possibility of the hull blistering when it's immersed for long periods. For other than trailered boats that are used for short periods, most boats' gelcoat below the waterline must be protected from water absorption by a waterproof coating.

Polyester is recommended for repairing any polyester product and can be applied to all surfaces except thermoplastics and oily woods. The resin is popular for structural repairs, such as gouged or deeply scraped topsides, where glass mat is required to impart high impact-resistance. The fiberglass gives polyester flexibility and impact-resistance. Polyester is generally less expensive than two-component epoxies and vinylesters. Proportions of polyester hardener, unlike epoxy, may be increased or decreased to allow ample work-time in high and low temperatures. It can be used over a broader range of temperatures than vinylester can. Polyesters will be tack-free in less than an hour and come to a full cure in less than six hours.

## VINYLESTER

Vinylester is the newest of the two-component resin systems. It cures by chemical reaction. It is recommended for structural repair and reinforcement of fiberglass. 3M MARINE WATER-BARRIER COATING is more waterproof than polyester, and also cures faster and sands more easily than epoxy does. Vinylester should not, however, be used over epoxy as there will be compatibility problems. It is effective above and below the waterline. One of its distinguishing characteristics is that it can be used for laminating fiberglass mat, and also as a finishing resin that will cure for easy sanding (see Laminating with Polyester, below). Vinylester resins gel in about 20 minutes and cure in 24 hours.

# One-Component Systems

Often simpler to use, sealants or adhesives made of just one component are also easier to clean up, but they generally have a slower cure time. There are a number of ways in which one-component systems cure. The type of cure can affect your choice of product.

▶ Systems that cure when the water they contain evaporates, such as ELMER'S GLUE.

▶ Systems that cure by the evaporation of a solvent, such as contact cements like 3M SPRAY TRIM ADHESIVE.

▶ Systems that cure by exposure to moisture—urethanes, and polysulfides such as 3M MARINE ADHESIVE SEALANT 5200 and 3M POLYSULFIDE MARINE SEALANT 101.

## SILICONE

3M MARINE GRADE MILDEW RESISTANT SILICONE is a one-component silicone-rubber sealant generally used above the waterline. Silicones are mildew-resistant and cure when exposed to ambient moisture. On application, they are nonsagging and remain flexible for years. Silicone adheres to metal, fiberglass, paint, glass, wood, most plastics, and rubber. I've often seen silicone used as a hose-gasket material under hose clamps. It is often used as window bedding and edge sealing, but be aware that silicone is not a strong adhesive and cannot be painted. Silicone is tack-free in five-to-10 minutes, and fully cured in 24 hours.

### POLYSULFIDE

**3M 101** and BoatLIFE LIFE CALK polysulfides are very popular one-component, pigmented sealants for use above and below the waterline. They're most often used as bedding compounds for deck hardware because they create excellent watertight seals. Polysulfide is compatible with metal, fiberglass, wood, concrete, and some plastics. If you need to seal ABS plastic, Lexan, or Plexiglas, don't use polysulfide—use a silicone product.

Polysulfides remain permanently flexible even where there is joint movement. They are resistant to salt water, weathering, and most chemicals. The don't sag and won't shrink. Old polysulfide is easier to remove than urethane sealants are when you're rebedding deck hardware. Most polysulfides are tack-free in less than five hours and cure fully in between five and 21 days.

### POLYURETHANE

**3M 5200** is extremely versatile and may be used in most applications above and below the waterline. It's a polyurethane, one-component, pigmented adhesive-sealant. The watertight seals it creates are nearly permanent, so you're likely to damage the substrate if you ever try to separate them. Think carefully before you apply a polyurethane adhesive-sealant. They are very strong and extremely tenacious on nonporous surfaces. Like most marine sealants, they are nonshrinking, nonsagging, and remain flexible after cure. Polyurethanes have excellent resistance to salt water and weathering. Most remain workable for up to four hours, become tack-free in 48 hours, and are fully cured in five to seven days.

**3M MARINE ADHESIVE SEALANT FAST CURE 4200** is a faster-curing urethane product that is tack-free in one hour and fully cured in 24 hours. Don't use it for structural strength, though, as you would **3M 5200**, because it's deliberately designed to be weaker (see below).

**3M 4200** and BoatLIFE SEAL were developed to solve the disadvantages of **3M 5200**, which is almost impossible to remove once it has cured. LIFE SEAL is a hybrid that contains polyurethane for adhesion and silicone for flexibility. You can use it on parts you may want to take apart later. **3M 4200** is a fast-curing, polyurethane sealant. It's also strong, but not as strong as **3M 5200**, which means you can take things apart more easily afterward.

### CYANOACRYLATE

You may know cyanoacrylate adhesives better as superglues. These single-component, clear adhesives are often used on nonporous materials requiring a very fast bond. PASCO-FIX or 3M QUICK FIX ADHESIVE can be applied to most rubbers, plastics, vinyls, wood, fiberglass, and metal. Cyanoacrylates have good resistance to chemicals, temperature changes, and shocks. They are not a good choice when you're looking for high strength *and* flexibility. Their fame comes from the instant adhesion obtained when two treated parts are joined. PASCO-FIX is primarily sold at boat shows or obtained directly from the manufacturer (941-627-9334). I've tried it on almost every surface imaginable and, most of the time, I'm astonished at how fast it works. Apply the clear liquid to each surface (except polyethylene and polypropylene), touch them together, and they are inseparable in less than seconds. Yes, I mean seconds. PASCO-FIX is able to join dissimilar products: wood to glass, for example, or rubber to metal. Twenty dollars for a few ounces sounds expensive, but if you use it a drop at a time, it seems to last forever.

### CONTACT ADHESIVES

Contact glues are single-component adhesives used for sticking carpeting, cloth, headliners, and silencing pads to metal, fiberglass, wood, and other trim materials. 3M SPRAY TRIM ADHESIVE creates immediate adhesion when two treated surfaces are joined. Unlike many other adhesives, contact glues can be used to bond Styrofoam to itself and to other materials.

### WOOD GLUES

Water-based wood adhesives, such as ELMER'S GLUE, are often used to bond two pieces of wood together when you don't need great adhesive strength. (Epoxy is generally used where exceptional bonding strength is needed.) Being neither water-resistant nor weather-resistant, wood glues are recommended primarily for interior projects, such as replacing a chip or splinter in the dinette. They're made with polyvinyl acetate resin and a plasticizer, and they cure rapidly as the water in them evaporates. They are very inexpensive compared to marine adhesives such as polyurethane or polysulfide. They may be cleaned up with water.

Unaffected by sunshine and moisture, resorcinol wood glue, made by Weldwood and other manufacturers, is a two-component adhesive that gives the best wood-to-wood bond available. For these reasons, resorcinol is used by custom wooden-boat builders and manufacturers of exterior-grade plywood in preference to epoxy, which is sensitive to water and light.

## The Right Stuff for the Job

For the marine market, there are five basic structural and repair resins used most often. Each resin has its advantages and disadvantages.

### *What to Use Where*

The following chart gives you suggestions about the resin (and sometimes the product) that will do the best job. Some individual products have

The Right Stuff for the Job

special or unusual characteristics that are noted with a numeral next to their brand name.

There are many more applications, but the following chart gives a good cross section of repairs and construction jobs. A star indicates the preferred product. A check mark identifies other products that will also do the job.

## Bedding Deck Hardware

Polysulfide sealants such as **3M 101** and BOATLIFE LIFE CALK are excellent for bedding deck hardware, through-hull fittings, ports, and hatches. They are usually the sealant of choice when a part may have to be removed later. Be sure there is an adequate backing plate somewhat larger than the deck fitting. Before applying the sealant, clean the dry surface thoroughly with acetone. Apply the sealant to a sound surface. The cure can be speeded up by spraying the sealant with water after you've applied it. Incidentally, don't overtighten the fitting's fasteners. Stop tightening before the sealant is squeezed out; then, after the sealant cures, you can tighten the fasteners down all the way.

## Repairing Gelcoat Scratches

You may find that using a rubbing compound, as suggested in chapter 2 on fiberglass, doesn't completely remove an imperfection in the gelcoat. In that case, try EVERCOAT PREMIUM GEL PASTE. It's a two-component polyester paste for repairing gelcoat scratches and gouges that do not penetrate all the way through the gelcoat. If the gouge penetrates right through to the glass, you may need to use epoxy or polyester with fiberglass cloth to repair it.

Prepare the surface by cleaning and drying it. Mix a small amount of colorant in the paste, so it will match the surrounding gelcoat color. Apply it to the damaged area and scrape it to a smooth surface. To obtain a glossy surface, cover the wet paste with a clear plastic film. After it's cured, sand it with 600-grit paper, buff it to a gloss, and wax it.

EVERCOAT GEL COAT SCRATCH PATCH is a one-component pigmented gelcoat paste that can repair small scratches and spider cracks. Spider cracks often occur around hinges and other small deck-mounted hardware parts that are not properly backed. If you plan to repair spider cracks, first correct the structural reason for the cracking by adding a backing plate or a fender washer that's slightly larger than the deck hardware.

Squeeze the paste from the tube into the crack. After 15 minutes, scrape off the excess paste flush with the deck. When it's cured, buff it and then wax it. Mineral spirits will clean up any unwanted residue.

## Laminating with Polyester

While this is not the place for detailed instructions on laminating layers of fiberglass and polyester, there is one important thing to remember about polyester resin: it's commonly available in two forms.

# Quick-Reference Application Chart

| APPLICATIONS | POLYURETHANE | POLYURETHANE HYBRID | POLYSULFIDE | SILICONE | EPOXY |
|---|---|---|---|---|---|
| | 3M 5200 (1), (4) | 3M 4200 (3) BoatLIFE Life Seal (3) | 3M 101 (2) BoatLIFE Life Calk (2) BoatLIFE Liquid Life Calk (2) | 3M (4) Evercoat (4) | West (1) Evercoat (1) Marine-Tex (1) |
| **Above Waterline** | | | | | |
| Sealant for large gaps | ★ | | | | ★ |
| Sealant for small gaps | ★ | ✔ | ✔ | | ★ |
| Structural repairs | ✔ | | | | ★ |
| Fairing surfaces | | | | | ★ |
| Gelcoat repairs | | | | | ✔ |
| Bedding deck hardware | ✔ | | ★ | | ✔ |
| Metal-to-wood adhesion | | | ★ | | ✔ |
| Paying wood deck seams | | | ★ | | |
| Gasketing windows | | ✔ | | ★ | |
| Glass-to-metal, wood, fiberglass | | ★ | | ✔ | |
| Adhesion to oily wood | | | ✔ (3M 101) | | |
| Electrical insulation | | ✔ | | ★ | |
| **Below Waterline** | | | | | |
| Sealant for large gaps | ★ | | | | ★ |
| Sealant for small gaps | ★ | | | | ★ |
| Structural adhesive | ★ | | | | ★ |
| Blister repair | ✔ | | | | ★ |
| Keel and hull fairing | ✔ | | | | ★ |
| Bedding seacocks | ✔ | | ★ | | |

1. Creates a permanent bond and is difficult to remove.
2. Not compatible with Lexan, Plexiglas, or ABS plastic.
3. Not compatible with oily wood.
4. Not suggested for wood deck seams.

★ = preferred product
✔ = usable product

Quick-Reference Application Chart

The Right Stuff for the Job

The first kind will not set hard unless you keep it covered with plastic to exclude air while it's curing. That means you can place the next layer on top, and create a chemical bond between the two. An example of a *laminating resin* like this is EVERCOAT POLYESTER LAMINATING RESIN.

The second type of polyester resin is known as a *finishing resin*, and it will cure to a hard finish. It's the final coat you put on top of the laminating resin. An example is EVERCOAT FIBERGLASS RESIN.

## Repairing Fiberglass with Epoxy

You can also laminate layers of fiberglass cloth with a two-part epoxy resin, or use epoxy resin with glass mat or cloth to fill holes in fiberglass. It's more expensive than polyester resin, but it's stronger and bonds better to cured polyester, which is used in most fiberglass hulls. WEST SYSTEM EPOXY and EVERCOAT EPOXY SYSTEMS, among others, have an extensive series of resins, fast and slow hardeners, and fillers, to adjust the strength and viscosity of the mix. WEST SYSTEM has a more expensive product line than others but in my opinion is the premium epoxy product on the market.

First, clean and dry the fiberglass surface thoroughly. Roughen shiny surfaces with sandpaper to improve adhesion. Mix the hardener and resin thoroughly in a number of small batches, rather than one large batch. That will give you more working time. Large batches will heat up and gel quickly. Apply the mix, either to the fiberglass itself or to fiberglass cloth. After application, remove any excess epoxy before it cures. Wipe tools off with acetone or lacquer thinner.

For high-strength putties, consider those made with epoxy. MARINE-TEX is sold as a two-part epoxy putty in kits of various sizes. It's found on most boats because it repairs almost anything. It's impervious to diesel fuel, gasoline, and many acids, alkalis, solvents, and chemicals, so it can be used nearly anywhere. Its compression strength of 8,000 pounds per square inch gives you a good idea of how tough the product is. MARINE-TEX cures under water, and it can be sanded, drilled, machined, painted, or stained. Before you use it, though, you should roughen the surface of the substrate with sandpaper to get the best bond. If you apply it under water, handle the putty with a piece of polyethylene plastic film so it doesn't stick to your hands while you are forcing it onto a wet surface.

Two companies, Polymeric Systems and Evercoat, produce epoxy putty sticks that can be used to make emergency repairs on metal, fiberglass, or almost any surface above or below the waterline. These epoxy-putty products come in tubes the shape of a cigar. There are different products for use on plastic, aluminum, metal, and wood.

Once again, rough-sand the substrate for the best bond. To use the putty, twist off an ample amount and knead it with your fingers until it is a uniform color. Within 15 or 20 minutes, stuff the putty into the area under repair, smooth the surface with water, and allow it to harden for about 45 minutes.

For minor repairs, the West System and Evercoat companies make small epoxy repair kits containing all you need: resin, hardener, silica and micro balloons for thickening, a syringe, stir-sticks, and even rubber gloves. Some kits include tubes of colorants.

And, easiest of all, are the epoxy strips made by Polymeric Systems. Whenever you need a very small amount of epoxy, place a POLYMERIC SYSTEM EPOXY STRIP on a hard surface and, beginning at the left end, roll a pencil along the strip, through succeeding pouches. The pencil first bursts a barrier between the resin and hardener, mixing as it rolls, and then pushes the mixed epoxy into a narrow point at the end. Cut the end and squeeze out a thimbleful of epoxy that is all mixed and ready to go.

Epoxy is normally used to repair delaminated fiberglass, such as an area of deck that has lost adhesion to its core. The object is to re-glue the delaminated layer to the solid core beneath. West System suggests drilling many holes in the surface, then injecting epoxy resin into each hole with a syringe. The core must be dry, of course. The laminate must then be weighted down or clamped until the epoxy cures.

## Using Sealants with Metals

Whenever a hole for a deck fitting is drilled in fiberglass, it's possible that water will enter the boat or penetrate into the core, no matter how well you bed the fitting. There are two ways to deal with this problem. If the hole is large, you can scrape away about a quarter-inch of balsa or plywood core all the way around the hole, leaving the fiberglass layers in place at top and bottom. Paint the exposed core with liquid epoxy resin to seal it, and, before it has cured completely, fill the gap you have made with epoxy putty.

Alternatively, if you are drilling a fairly small hole through the deck to take a bolt, drill the hole about an eighth of an inch larger than needed. Seal the bottom of the hole with masking tape temporarily and fill it with epoxy resin. When the epoxy has cured, drill the correct-sized hole down through the middle of the epoxy.

You can use **3M 101**, **3M 5200**, or BOATLIFE LIFE CALK to coat the threads of a screw or bolt you're fastening through fiberglass. All deck fittings need bedding compound beneath them, of course, but it's also a good policy to dip the screw point into the sealant. When the screw is driven into place, the sealant will ride up the screw and form a gasket on the threads and beneath the screw top. This seal will make the hole leakproof. The sealant also acts as a barrier to galvanic action between two dissimilar metals.

And next time you need to attach a cleat or block to an aluminum mast with pop rivets, put a small quantity of **3M 4200** or BOATLIFE LIFE CALK on the pop rivet before it is driven into the metal, just as you would with screws and bolts.

EVERCOAT ALUMINOX EPOXY STICKS will fill small holes on oxidized and anodized aluminum surfaces. The epoxy will grip better if you roughen the surface before application. If you're applying the stuff under water, use the polyethylene wrapper so the epoxy doesn't stick to your hands. Sometimes you'll need to etch the surface of aluminum before you can bond it with epoxy. West System makes a two-part aluminum etching kit for preparing the metal.

Finally, FASTSTEEL STEEL REINFORCED EPOXY PUTTY is a hand-kneadable, nonrusting, steel-reinforced putty for repairing any metal product. The putty contains microscopic steel platelets for strength. It can be drilled, tapped, machined, sanded, and filed. Roughen the metal surface before application. The repaired part can be put back in service in one hour.

## Uses for Urethanes and Silicones

**Urethane:** 3M 5200 is a urethane adhesive and sealant that can be used above or below the waterline. Its advantage over other sealants is in the incredible strength generated at the bond between two nonporous surfaces. This bond is so strong that if separation of the surfaces is required some day, the substrate may be damaged during removal. 3M 5200 is therefore erroneously used in applications where weaker polysulfides are better suited. Pure urethanes like 3M 5200 should be used in structural applications, such as hull-to-deck seams, or those uses where removal is very unlikely. If in doubt, use a polysulfide.

**Hybrid urethane:** BOATLIFE LIFE SEAL is a hybrid combination of urethane and silicone. The addition of silicone reduces the bond strength of the urethane, allowing the sealant to be removed at some later date, if necessary, and gives LIFE SEAL the ability to adhere to glass and plastic surfaces. LIFE SEAL has adhesive qualities in the same range as polysulfides like 3M 101 or BOATLIFE LIFE CALK. It has become an industry standard for sealing glass and most plastics to a full range of surfaces.

**Silicone:** 3M MARINE GRADE MILDEW RESISTANT SILICONE is a popular silicone product. I would restrict the application of silicone to its main use as a sealant for Lexan windows, plus a few unusual jobs, such as blunting the sharp ends of cotter pins and forming a hose gasket beneath stainless-steel clamps. Silicone has rather poor adhesive properties, and does not have the long life of sealants like LIFE SEAL that can be more successfully used for other plastic adhesive applications.

## Other Materials

### PLASTIC

POLYMERIC SYSTEM QUIKPLASTIK EPOXY PUTTY PLASTIC ADHESIVE is a hand-kneadable putty that bonds to all plastic surfaces except polyethylene and polypropylene. Mold it to shape for any repair on rigid or semi-rigid plastic. After two or three hours, the part can be put back in service.

BOATLIFE LIFE SEAL seals glass and most plastics to many surfaces. 3M MARINE GRADE MILDEW RESISTANT SILICONE is often selected to give a waterproof seal around the edges of plastic windows and ports.

## INFLATABLES

Inflatable dinghies often develop slow leaks as they age. Many of the leaks are in the inflating valves, but often, small leaks occur in the fabric and seams of the boat. Push the suspicious part of the boat under water when it's fully inflated and look for telltale bubbles, or brush a soapy solution all over and look for bubbles. Determine if the inflatable is made from PVC or Hypalon fabric; that will direct you to the correct adhesive. If possible, abrade the damaged area and apply a patch using one of the many kits available for your boat's fabric.

It is not easy to tell a Hypalon dinghy from a PVC dinghy unless they are side by side. Hypalon inflatables are without exception more costly and have long warranties, often up to 10 years. Hypalon boats are hand-crafted with either butted or lapped seams covered with a tape. PVC boats are far less expensive and usually have only a five-year warranty. Most PVC seams are welded, and become quite brittle after long exposure.

If you cannot determine the type of fabric, try POLYMARINE INFLATABLE BOAT PATCH ADHESIVE #3026. This is a two-part urethane adhesive that is designed to glue patches to all types of fabrics used on inflatable boats.

However, if you are certain you have a Hypalon boat, use POLYMARINE #2990 HYPALON ADHESIVE. Otherwise, temporary repairs can be made with patch kits containing one-component contact cement.

When all else fails, try INLAND MARINE INFLATABLE SEALANT. Deflate the boat. Squirt a few ounces of the sealant into an open valve. Inflate the boat, and rotate it so the sealant coats the inside of the tubes. Repeat the procedure if the first application fails to stop the leaks. This method gets at those small holes too little to detect with the naked eye, or with a bubble test.

For larger repair jobs, try INLAND MARINE INFLATABLE RUBBER. This is a two-part rubber with the consistency of honey. It can be used for reinforcing inflatable skins or for capping dock pilings. It's easy to use: abrade the fabric, then clean and dry it. Mix the components, and, after waiting one hour, roll or brush the mix onto the inflatable. The mix has a pot life of between four and six hours. It dries tack-free in two days and cures fully in seven days. There's one thing to watch: it won't cure in temperatures below 70°F. You can, however, accelerate the cure by blowing hot air from a hair dryer on the surface.

## HEADLINERS

After years of exposure, the foam backing on fabric headliners in the cabin may disintegrate, and the liner will come loose from the bulkhead. But you can reattach it this way:

Mask off any nearby painted or varnished areas. Clean and dry the surface before application. Spray 3M SPRAY TRIM ADHESIVE onto both surfaces in overlapping sweeps. Give it at least five minutes to dry before joining the two surfaces, but be sure to join them within one hour. Apply pressure to get a strong seal.

### HOSES

**3M MARINE GRADE MILDEW RESISTANT SILICONE** is often used as a gasket material at hose clamps. Clean and dry the surface. Apply the silicone between the hose and the barb. Attach the hose to the barb. Tighten the stainless hose clamp. A good, waterproof seal is created at the clamped area. Remove any excess at once.

**EVERCOAT GASKET MAKER AND SEALER** is a natural rubber gasket compound that bonds to metal surfaces and remains flexible. It is very resistant to chemicals and fuel. You can use it to make temporary gaskets on carburetors, hoses, and pumps. It also bonds to canvas, vinyl, and rubber. Apply two coats and wait an hour before putting the part into service.

### VINYL

You'll find many liquid vinyl-repair products at hardware, automotive, and marine stores. **VLP CLEAR LIQUID VINYL REPAIR** is one that works well to repair cracks in vinyl seat cushions and boat tops.

For short tears, apply a thin layer, a half-inch wide, along the tear and let it dry for 30 minutes. Then apply a second layer.

For long tears, hold the tear together with masking tape every two inches. Apply layers of VLP in the nontaped areas as above. When it has cured, remove the tape and apply layers in those areas where the tape was removed. Allow four hours before putting it back in use.

If you want a nonglossy finish, apply a little VLP to a lint-free cloth and dab it lightly onto the cured repair until the gloss disappears.

### RESCUING ROTTING WOOD

Wood may rot when the moisture content in the fibers reaches 40 percent. At this point, a fungus may begin to digest the wood cellulose, and decomposition begins. The longer the fungus is allowed to remain, the more wood fiber will be destroyed. There are only two ways to deal with this: replace the wood, or inject epoxy into the wood to replace the destroyed fibers.

**GIT-ROT** is a two-part epoxy resin that has a very liquid consistency, allowing it to seep into rotten fibers, fill the voids and rejuvenate the wood.

To locate dry rot, tap questionable areas with a hammer and listen for a hollow, dead sound. Probe those areas with an ice pick to determine if the wood is solid.

The wood must be dry for the epoxy to work effectively. If there's any doubt, dry as much as possible before proceeding. Soaking the rotten wood with acetone will assist drying, but be careful, it's highly flammable.

Drill many holes in the rotten wood surface or end-grain so the epoxy can soak right through. Since it is hard to pour liquid into small holes, put a straw into the GIT-ROT. Then place a finger over the top of the filled straw, transfer it to the hole, and release the right amount of epoxy by lifting your finger. Replace your finger, and move to the next hole. Don't leave smears on the surface—they'll be difficult to remove when they've cured. Mix some sawdust into GIT-ROT to fill larger, open areas.

ELECTRICAL CONNECTIONS

Try using WEST MARINE LIQUID ELECTRICAL TAPE or MDR LIQUID LECTRIC TAPE in place of electric tape when you're sealing electrical connections. These products are viscous black, water-based, liquid-vinyl sealants. They seal and protect electrical connections, and prevent corrosion in moist conditions by forming a tough dielectric coating that keeps out dirt and moisture better than electric tape or shrink-tubing does.

Clean and dry the contact area. Brush the liquid tape onto the connection. After the first coat dries, in approximately 30 minutes, apply a second coat, and a third one if you need to build up thickness. Any excess can be cleaned up with water.

# Quick-Reference Guide
## Sealants and Adhesives

| MATERIAL | TOPIC | JOB | PAGE | PRODUCT | HOW TO DO JOB |
|---|---|---|---|---|---|
| **Fiberglass** | Structural | Permanent installations | 92, 98 | **3M MARINE ADHESIVE SEALANT 5200** | Clean surface. Apply **5200**. Partially tighten fasteners. When tack-free, tighten down all the way. Clean up excess before cures. |
| | Bedding hardware | Deck hardware | 94 | **3M POLYSULFIDE MARINE SEALANT 101; BOATLIFE LIFE CALK** | Clean with acetone. Apply sealant. Partially tighten fasteners. When cured, tighten down all the way. |
| | Small gelcoat repairs | Cuts, gouges | 94 | **EVERCOAT PREMIUM GEL PASTE** | Clean. Mix colorant into paste. Apply to damaged area and smooth. Buff to gloss and wax. |
| | | Scratches | 94 | **EVERCOAT GEL COAT SCRATCH PATCH** | Squeeze paste into scratch. Scrape off excess. After cure, buff and wax. |
| | Small lamination repairs | | 96 | **EVERCOAT LAMINATING POLYESTER RESIN; EVERCOAT FIBERGLASS RESIN** | Clean. Lay on fiberglass mat. Apply polyester mix. Use finishing resin and hardener for final coat. Sand. Apply gelcoat or paint. |

*continues*

Quick-Reference Guide

## Sealants and Adhesives (continued)

| MATERIAL | TOPIC | JOB | PAGE | PRODUCT | HOW TO DO JOB |
|---|---|---|---|---|---|
| **Fiberglass ctd.** | Composite construction | Construction and repair | 96 | WEST SYSTEM EPOXY | Clean. Sand. Lay on fiberglass cloth. Apply epoxy mix. Multiple layers if required. |
| | | Small repairs | 96, 97 | MARINE-TEX; POLYMERIC SYSTEM EPOXY STRIP | Clean. Sand. Apply putty. Smooth off surface with wet finger. |
| **Metal** | Stainless steel | Screws and bolts | 97 | 3M POLYSULFIDE MARINE SEALANT 101; 3M MARINE ADHESIVE SEALANT 5200; BOATLIFE LIFE CALK | Wipe screw with sealant. Drive into screw hole. Back off, then seat screw. |
| | Aluminum | Pop rivets | 97 | 3M MARINE ADHESIVE SEALANT FAST CURE 4200; BOATLIFE LIFE CALK | Wipe pop rivet with sealant before it is nailed into the metal. |
| **Plastic** | Rigid or semi-rigid | Repair | 98 | POLYMERIC SYSTEM QUIKPLASTIK EPOXY PUTTY PLASTIC ADHESIVE | Clean, dry, and roughen surface. Knead putty. Apply to rigid or semi-rigid plastic surface. Apply pressure. |
| | Plastic to other surfaces | Bonding | 98 | BOATLIFE LIFE SEAL | Clean and dry surface. Apply thin layer to both surfaces. Join with pressure. |
| | Lexan | Bonding | 98 | 3M MARINE GRADE MILDEW RESISTANT SILICONE | Clean surfaces to bond. Apply bead of sealant. Tighten fasteners. Clean up excess. |

| MATERIAL | TOPIC | JOB | PAGE | PRODUCT | HOW TO DO JOB |
|---|---|---|---|---|---|
| **Fabric** | Inflatable dinghy | Repair tears | 99 | POLYMARINE INFLATABLE BOAT PATCH ADHESIVE #3026 | Clean. Abrade surface. Apply 2-part urethane adhesive to both surfaces. Bond them with pressure if possible. |
| | | Repair leaks | 99 | INLAND MARINE INFLATABLE SEALANT | Deflate boat. Squirt into each flotation unit. Inflate boat. Rotate boat. |
| | | Large repairs | 99 | INLAND MARINE INFLATABLE RUBBER | Abrade fabric. Clean. Roll or brush sealant onto fabric. |
| | Headliner | Re-attaching | 99 | 3M SPRAY TRIM ADHESIVE | Mask adjoining areas. Clean and dry. Spray adhesive on both surfaces. Join after 5 minutes and apply pressure. |
| | Hose | Gasketing | 100 | 3M MARINE GRADE MILDEW RESISTANT SILICONE; EVERCOAT GASKET MAKER AND SEALER | Clean and dry. Apply **3M SILICONE** to hose barb. Attach hose and stainless clamp. **EVERCOAT GASKET MAKER** creates temporary carburetor, hose, and pump gaskets. |
| | Vinyl | Vinyl rip repair | 100 | VLP CLEAR LIQUID VINYL REPAIR | Clean and dry. Apply paste to rip. |
| **Wood** | Rotten wood | Repair | 100 | BOATLIFE GIT-ROT | Dry wood. Drill holes in rotted areas. Pour epoxy into holes. Sand when cured. Apply protective coating. |
| **Electrical** | Electric tape | Moisture and corrosion seal | 101 | WEST MARINE LIQUID ELECTRICAL TAPE; MDR LIQUID LECTRIC TAPE | Clean and dry. Brush liquid onto connection. Apply 2 more coats. |

# 7
# FABRIC

**F**abric stains should be treated quickly. Keep stains wet for as long as possible, as you'll have more success if you work on spots that have not dried out. Try rinsing stains with cold water first. Greasy stains need to be saturated with a liquid detergent like SPRAY 'N WASH followed by a water rinse. Bad stains may respond to a cleaning fluid like nail-polish remover, or even acetone, with an absorbent fabric placed beneath the stain. Nongreasy stains should be sponged with cold water as soon as possible, then soaked in cold water for a minimum of 30 minutes.

Most fabric-cleaning failures occur because the soaking part of the process is rushed. Give a cleanser such as WOOLITE its full recommended soak time and you'll usually be successful. As a general rule, blot stains up and down. Don't rub them from side to side.

## Acrylic Fabric

If it's at all possible, rinse your dodger and bimini (which are likely to be made of a material such as SUNBRELLA), with freshwater after every excursion. Salt crystals will hold moisture on the fabric indefinitely. When you must do more than just rinse, the manufacturer of SUNBRELLA recommends washing it with a solution of water and bleach. Try a 20-to-1 ratio. If the fabric is colored, they suggest using CLOROX 2.

To waterproof an acrylic fabric such as SUNBRELLA, first clean it and dry it, then waterproof the fabric with APSEAL or 303 FABRIC GUARD. These aerosol waterproofers are not always easy to find. Keep the overspray from both products away from fiberglass or PLEXIGLAS as the solvents in the compound can harm them. If you can, remove the fabric to be treated from the boat and spread it out on shore. 303 FABRIC GUARD is the only water repellent recommended by the manufacturer of SUNBRELLA. Applied properly, it can last as long as three years. If you prefer not to spray, paint on one of the liquid waterproofers like STAR BRITE WATERPROOFING AND FABRIC TREATMENT using a two-inch-wide foam brush, which makes it easy to soak large pieces of SUNBRELLA.

## Dacron

Care will add years to the life of a Dacron sail. One of the main causes of sailcloth failure is imbedded dirt rubbing away at the fibers. Dirt is attracted by salt, which itself is highly abrasive and holds moisture. If you don't fully dry your sails, you'll invite mildew to form on the dirt embedded in them. For these reasons, it's a good idea to remove the salt with a freshwater rinse.

Clean sails with freshwater, dry them, and store them in a manner that minimizes the amount of creases. Stains will require gentle scrubbing on a flat surface using a very mild cleanser such as BOAT ZOAP, then rinsing. If required, spot-clean with CLOROX 2, not regular bleach. The active ingredients in CLOROX 2 are hydrogen peroxide and surfactants, not chlorine, which can harm sail fabric. Rinse thoroughly with cold water.

If the sails are badly soiled, you can remove dirt by washing them with household detergent and water. It's important to rinse the sail very thoroughly afterward, as the alkaline ingredients in household detergents will damage DACRON. Dry the sail on a clothesline if possible. Remember, however, that washing a sail with detergent will remove some or all of the sizing that is there to stiffen the sail and treat its surface. If you can accept the cost, have a sailmaker clean the sails and resize them.

### Lubricating Sail Tracks

I lubricate sail slides with a clear lubricant called FASTRAC for easier handling. Apply it to sail tracks to ease the raising and lowering of sails. Unlike other lubricants, FASTRAC does not attract dirt. You can also purchase a cleaner/applicator from the same company. The applicator fits all sizes of track, and can be hauled up the mast on a halyard and then pulled back down with a lanyard. It cleans and lubricates as it goes.

### OIL OR GREASE STAINS

First try to scrape excess tar or grease off the sail. Carefully apply a conventional solvent fabric cleaner to remove the remaining stain. Follow with a detergent wash on the treated area and rinse thoroughly.

When removing small spots, you won't need to be concerned about removing the sizing. This only needs to be addressed if the whole sail is washed with detergent.

Suntan lotion is worth special mention. One calm afternoon, when I was motoring in my boat, an overly oiled guest used the flaked-down genoa as a pillow. A perfect body outline of suntan lotion was transferred to the sail. SPRAY 'N WASH did the trick of getting it off.

### RUST STAINS

If possible, try to keep the rusted sail area wet. As a start, try to clean it with lemon juice. If that doesn't work, scrub the spot carefully with a detergent.

As a last resort, apply a solution of water and BAR KEEPERS FRIEND, which contains oxalic acid. Rinse thoroughly with fresh water.

## MILDEW

Try using lemon juice on the mildewed part of the sail. Conventional chlorine bleach is not good for DACRON as its high alkalinity is destructive to the fibers. Rinse, then leave to dry in the sun and fresh air.

## BLOODSTAINS

It isn't within the scope of this book to try to describe all the ways blood gets on sails. Let it be enough to say that the foredeck handler often gets blood on the sail while wrestling it to the deck and into the bag. Fresh blood can be removed easily with a long rinse under running cold water. Old, dried bloodstains may need a dab of diluted ammonia before the cold rinse.

---

### Temporary Sail Repair

Special sticky-back tapes, found in marine stores, work well to temporarily heal a ripped sail. MARINERS CHOICE SAIL BANDAGE, a high-strength, waterproof, translucent, adhesive tape, can do the job. You can apply it on rips in wet sails to make an emergency repair, and when you make permanent repairs, you can sew right through the temporary tape.

---

# Neoprene and Hypalon

Synthetic rubber coatings called neoprene and HYPALON are used in the construction of inflatable boats. Combined with fabric, they make an extremely tough and lightweight composite.

## Cleaning Inflatables

Last summer, it seemed more convenient for me to leave my inflatable dinghy in the water tied to my boat than to manhandle it onto my deck or row it to the dinghy storage dock 200 yards away. What I hadn't counted on was the high salinity caused by a drought, plus the high water temperature brought on by a prolonged heat wave. These were conditions perfectly suited for living organisms to find a home on the dinghy bottom. Within two months, the bottom was covered with zebra mussels and barnacles. Slime and grass filled the spaces in between.

The first step was to power-wash the bottom. Most of the slime and grass, and some zebra mussels, came off. The next step was to remove the barnacles and mussels with an instrument that would not cut the dinghy fabric. I tried scraping them off with blocks of wood, window ice scrapers, and a dull putty knife. All were successful in removing the living shells but what remained were the adhesive anchors better known as barnacle rings. The real task

---

### Kevlar

KEVLAR is a special high-tech sail material usually found on racing sailboats. Don't use detergents when washing it. They can damage the fabric. Rinse only with copious amounts of water, even when you are just spot-cleaning. Stories circulate that KEVLAR fibers are tougher than steel. Conventional methods of cutting fabric don't work on KEVLAR, but if you persevere, you can cut it with a serrated blade.

---

began when I started the laborious process of scraping off the barnacle rings. Acid-containing cleaners like BAR KEEPERS FRIEND or ON & OFF did a decent job of softening the rings. Spraying lemon juice and vinegar onto the still-wet bottom has also been recommended. I then used the dull putty knife, held at about a 75-degree angle, to scrape them off one at a time. After a very thorough rinse the bottom was almost like new. However, ON & OFF has such a highly effective acid component that it took much of the color out of the fabric of my orange dinghy. On the other hand, the barnacle rings are gone.

The barnacles and mussels are much easier to remove when they are wet and alive, compared to when they are dead. The calcified rings come off quite easily if they're scraped soon after knocking off the barnacles. When they dry out, the rings are brittle and more difficult to remove. It's therefore a good idea to do only as much of the bottom as you can get to in the time allotted, keeping the remaining area wet and intact until you can finish the job.

For less drastic cleaning, STAR BRITE INFLATABLE BOAT AND FENDER CLEANER/PROTECTOR or MARYKATE INFLATABLE BOAT CLEANER both do a good job of getting dirt, food, and dried-on scum off the inflatable. They are specially formulated to clean the fabric without harsh scrubbing. To remove stains from inflatable fabric in otherwise good condition, wash them with a strong solution of bleach and water. Use rubber gloves when you scrub. After rinsing, put on a quality wax or, if necessary, protect the fabric by painting on MDR INFLATABLE AND DINGHY BOTTOM COATING.

## Antifouling Paint for Inflatables

Someone finally brought out a good inflatable bottom coating: MDR INFLATABLE AND DINGHY BOTTOM COATING is a water-based antifouling coating containing cuprous oxide. Follow the instructions and don't use it on an aluminum dinghy bottom, as the cuprous oxide and aluminum are not compatible. No primer is needed. It can be brushed onto a clean inflatable bottom to discourage marine growth on dinghies that spend their summers in the water. It is environmentally safe.

# Carpet

One of the problems with fabric stains is that there is no one product that will safely remove all types. No two stains are exactly alike. For this reason, there will be many differing solutions. As an example CARBONA has developed a series of 10 different stain removers in small bottles called STAIN DEVILS to cover the most prevalent stains. The whole series can be obtained in supermarkets.

For routine cleaning of a carpeted cabin, try using a small, short-handled, manual carpet sweeper. The short handle makes it easy to clean the floor in tight quarters. Automotive store foam carpet cleaners like BLUE

Coral Dri-Clean Carpet and Upholstery Cleaner, at around $3 per can, are good for removing most mild stains. On severe food stains, use a commercial foam cleaner that can be purchased at vacuum-cleaner stores. Resist the temptation to scrub foam cleaners vigorously, as the carpet fibers will easily abrade.

To remove mud stains, cover them with salt, sprinkle water on the salt, and vacuum when it's dry. With truly stubborn unidentified stains, go for a cleaning fluid like nail-polish remover or acetone. Sponge the spot with the cleaning fluid after testing color fastness on a hidden corner.

Oil-based paint stains can be removed from carpet. Scrape off what you can, then sponge very carefully with acetone. Again, test for carpet color-fastness by trying acetone in a hidden corner before you commit yourself to the actual spot of soil, which will almost always be in the dead center of your carpet.

# Upholstery

If you vacuum the boat upholstery often, it will minimize the normal build-up of dirt stains. Cleaning will be easier if you don't let dirt get embedded in the fibers in the first place.

Spray 'n Wash spot remover does a good job of removing a variety of stains from cloth. Blue Coral Dri-Clean Carpet and Upholstery Cleaner can be used if a foam cleaner is preferred.

### Wine stains

Start working on the stain while it's still wet. Apply white wine or sparkling water generously to a red wine spill. Soak up as much as possible with paper towels. Once the stain is mostly gone, a good upholstery cleaner like Blue Coral Dri-Clean Carpet and Upholstery Cleaner can usually finish the job.

### Wax

Scrape off the excess wax. Place absorbent cloth toweling on both sides of the fabric and touch with a warm iron. The wax, made fluid by the heat, should flow out of the cloth and into the absorbent towel.

### Tar

Scrape off what you can. If possible, apply cooking oil to the tar, which will loosen it from the fabric, then sponge it with a cleaning fluid such as nail-polish remover or acetone. Work inward from the outside, to try to prevent making a ring. As always, color-test first.

### Rust

Color-test the fabric before you proceed. Apply bleach or lemon juice to the rusted spot. If you can safely introduce steam from an iron, it will help. Rinse and repeat as often as necessary.

# Footwear and Boat Clothing

Damp shoes develop bad smells. Sew cedar chips into a sock and slip the tube into each shoe for an overnight treat. The shoes will, hopefully, smell as good as new in the morning. Shake baking soda into shoes that are beyond hope. It's always worth a try to save a favorite pair.

Shoes soaked with salt water never seem to dry. To get rid of the salt, immerse them in potable water. Adding white vinegar to the water will more aggressively remove the salt. Stuff the insides with paper towels and air-dry them without using heat. You might want to let them dry in the sun. Use saddle soap or neat's-foot oil to soften the dry leather. If they shrink, rub the tight spots with alcohol, and put the shoes on while the treated area is still wet. Vodka is almost pure alcohol and will soften the tight spot just as well as cleaning alcohol will, if you can spare a small amount from cocktail hour. When you've finished, polish the shoes to protect the leather.

Mildew and dried salt are the major problems you will encounter with clothing on the boat. Fleece garments are the current wonder of the clothing age. A cold-water machine wash is all that is needed to bring them back to like-new condition. GORE-TEX is a popular waterproof and breathable fabric used in many boating garments. It can be kept clean by machine washing in a nondetergent soap like IVORY FLAKES or DREFT.

Conventional foul-weather gear is made of a PVC, urethane, or neoprene coating, often laminated onto a nylon shell. After wearing them in bad weather, rinse them off to remove salt water. Don't store them wet. Hang them to dry on a wooden hanger to prevent rust stains. Never put foul-weather gear in a washer or dryer. You can remove stains with a mild cleanser, such as DREFT or IVORY FLAKES.

## Treat Spots Before Washing

You already have MURPHY'S OIL SOAP on the boat. Dab some on clothing stains before you wash them. It's a good pre-spotter and will clear away most stains.

# Quick-Reference Guide

## Fabric

| TOPIC | JOB | PAGE | PRODUCT | HOW TO DO JOB |
|---|---|---|---|---|
| **Acrylic** | Cleaning | 105 | CLOROX 2 | Rinse with freshwater. If soiled severely, wash with CLOROX 2, rinse. |
| | Waterproofing | 105 | APSEAL; 303 FABRIC GUARD | Apply to clean, dry fabric. Allow to dry before reinstalling covers. |
| **Dacron** | Cleaning sails | 106 | CLOROX 2 | Clean with freshwater. If required, spot clean with CLOROX 2. Rinse well. |
| | Removing grease or oil | 106 | Solvent cleaner | Scrape off excess. Apply solvent cleaner. Detergent wash. Rinse well. |
| | Suntan lotion | 106 | SPRAY 'N WASH | Wet sail. Apply SPRAY 'N WASH and rinse thoroughly. Dry in sun. |
| | Removing rust | 106–107 | Lemon juice; oxalic acid | Rinse stain with lemon juice. If required, apply mild oxalic acid. Rinse well. |
| | Removing mildew | 107 | Lemon juice | Apply lemon juice to spot. Let dry in sun. |
| | Bloodstains | 107 | Diluted ammonia | Rinse fresh bloodstains with cold water. Old stains need a dab of ammonia, then a cold rinse. |
| **Kevlar** | Cleaning | 107 | Water | Do not use detergent. Use only water to clean. |
| **Neoprene and Hypalon** | Cleaning | 108 | STAR BRITE INFLATABLE BOAT AND FENDER CLEANER/ PROTECTOR; MARYKATE INFLATABLE BOAT CLEANER | Apply inflatable boat cleaner. Don't scrub hard enough to abrade fabric. |
| | Coating | 108 | MDR INFLATABLE AND DINGHY BOTTOM COATING | Brush onto a clean inflatable bottom. |
| | Removing barnacles | 108 | MARYKATE ON & OFF HULL AND BOTTOM CLEANER | Applied, the cleaner will soften the barnacle rings, allowing easier removal by soft scraping. |

*continues*

# Quick-Reference Guide

## Fabric (continued)

| Topic | Job | Page | Product | How to Do Job |
|---|---|---|---|---|
| **Neoprene and Hypalon, ctd.** | Stains | 108 | Bleach; **MDR Inflatable and Dinghy Bottom Coating** | Wash with water and bleach solution. Apply wax or coat with **MDR** bottom coating. |
| **Carpet** | Cleaning | 108–109 | **Blue Coral Dri-Clean Carpet and Upholstery Cleaner** | Follow manufacturer's directions. |
| | Removing mud | 109 | Salt | Apply salt to stain and wet area. Vacuum when dry. |
| | Removing oil paint | 109 | Acetone | Scrape off excess. Test for color fastness with acetone. Sponge carefully with acetone to remove paint. |
| **Upholstery** | General stains | 109 | **Spray 'n Wash** | Test for color fastness. Apply as needed. |
| | Wine stain | 109 | White wine | Keep wet. Apply white wine to red wine stain. Blot with paper towels. Follow with upholstery cleaner. |
| | Removing wax | 109 | Cloth towels; iron | Scrape off excess wax. Cover with towel. Touch towel with hot iron. |
| | Removing tar | 109 | Cleaning fluid | Color-test. Scrape off excess tar. Sponge with cleaning fluid. |
| | Removing rust | 109 | Lemon juice | Color-test. Apply lemon juice to rust. Carefully apply steam from iron. Rinse. |
| **Clothing** | Salty shoes | 110 | White vinegar; neat's-foot oil | Soak shoes in fresh water and white vinegar. Stuff with paper. Dry in sun. Apply neat's-foot oil to soften leather. Polish with shoe polish. |
| | Spot cleaning | 110 | **Murphy's Oil Soap** | Spot stains with **Murphy's Oil Soap**, then clean as usual. |
| | Foul-weather gear | 110 | **Ivory Flakes; Dreft** | Rinse with fresh water. Remove stains with cleaner. |

# 8

# PLASTIC, VINYL, LINE, AND RUBBER

## Plastic

In the future, an increasing number of marine parts will be made of engineered plastic, because of its high strength, light weight, and excellent resistance to corrosion. Tremendous strides have been made by means of the alloying process to create products that will last indefinitely. Incidentally, what we call corrosion in metals is called degradation in plastics.

Some of the more common plastics used for boat parts are nylon, DELRIN, TEFLON, LEXAN, and acrylic plastic. Vinyl and polyester gelcoat can be considered plastics but, because of their nonstructural uses, they are not defined as engineering-grade plastics.

### Plastics Used on Boats

Nylon is a tough, engineering-grade plastic. It is strong in tension, under impact, and while flexing. It is highly resistant to abrasion and not affected by most chemicals. It is used for bearings, gears, cams, and rollers because it machines easily, like brass. MARELON is the trade name for a composite of nylon and glass fibers that is often used in seacocks and pipe fittings. Drilling nylon requires care because the bit produces considerable heat and can melt the plastic. Use bits that are highly polished and have a long lead. Withdraw the drill from the hole frequently to cool off the bit.

DELRIN is a resin with physical properties that bridge the gap between metals and plastics. Delrin also machines easily.

TEFLON is used in a wide range of products because it has a very low friction coefficient: it's as slippery as ice on ice. This characteristic makes TEFLON excellent for bearings and seals. It swells slightly when you drill into it, which makes the drilled hole smaller than the bit; so use a slightly larger bit than the hole you want to make.

Acrylic plastics such as LUCITE and PLEXIGLAS are easy to machine and polish. So is a polycarbonate such as LEXAN. Used primarily in place of glass for hatches and ports, acrylics and polycarbonate have high impact resistance and are available in clear or smoked shades. They are drilled in the same way as other plastics, using sharp bits with long leads. If you need to drill a smooth-walled hole, create a pilot hole and fill it with wax. That will help the chips move up the flutes without sticking to the drill.

Vinyl is a plasticized polyvinyl chloride (PVC). The plasticizer makes it flexible. Vinyl, therefore, is a good choice for windows that roll up. But because it is soft, vinyl is easily damaged. It is not as clear as LEXAN or the acrylic plastics that are commonly used for rigid windows. Due to its unique characteristics and many applications on the boat, I have treated vinyl below in its own category.

Most marine products made with nylon, DELRIN, and TEFLON will be invisible in use, forming bearings, cams, and seals. You'll find instructions for cleaning these plastics in the manufacturer's pamphlets. Winches and jam cleats are examples of products that may be made from these plastics. Usually, a good freshwater rinse between regular maintenance is all that will be needed.

MARELON, a fiberglass-reinforced nylon, is often used for cleats, seacocks, and replacements for bronze fittings. Wiping it down occasionally with a rag soaked in BOAT ZOAP will usually suffice to keep it clean.

## Taking Care of Plastic

Like anything else on your boat, components made of plastic need occasional care and maintenance. Here are some useful tips for most of the types of marine plastic. The exception is vinyl, which has a section of its own, below.

Before attempting to clean plastic, consider that acrylic, LEXAN, PLEXIGLAS, and other "soft" plastics are more easily damaged than metal is, so be careful when cleaning. Paper towels and stiff brushes can scratch their surfaces. The best material to use for cleaning is a soft cotton T-shirt.

For general cleaning, use an inexpensive solution of water and white vinegar. WINDEX also does an excellent job of cleaning these plastics as well as glass. Realize that strong cleaners can etch the softer plastic surfaces.

Crazing refers to the web-like scratches that appear, as if by magic, on plastic. Crazing creates small cuts or grooves in the plastic surface. The first line of defense is to apply a good polish like STAR BRITE PREMIUM MARINE POLISH WITH TEFLON. This temporarily fills the scratch with polymer, which, in turn, reduces light refraction and minimizes the crazing.

Mild polishes like the MICROMESH system can be used to buff out severe scratches. It is, however, a tedious job of working up through ascending grit levels to a final buffing with an abrasive sheet almost as smooth as cloth.

If you don't have the patience to attempt the MICROMESH system, you may want to attempt one more procedure. This may be a last-ditch effort before replacing the plastic piece. Pick a small, unobtrusive corner. Buff it with BRASSO or NOXON 7 with bronze wool. Wait a few days before you proceed to be sure you are not doing further damage with these abrasive products. Exposure to the weather will reveal if the polish has done more harm than good to the plastic surface.

Once in a while, in an old port or hatch, the crazing will be internal. Little can be done, short of replacing the entire piece, when the crazing is this extreme.

Though acrylic and LEXAN are not difficult to drill, you may not have the equipment to cut out an exact shape. It's best left to the professionals. Large commercial plastic suppliers have the correct cutting and drilling equipment, plus the expertise to cut the plastic sheet and drill holes for an exact match. Give them the old piece as a pattern.

## Making Plastic Water-Repellent

A water-beading coating called **RAIN X**, when applied to glass or plastic windows, prevents steaming and improves visibility in heavy rain. The micro-polymer formulation cleans, polishes, and coats the surface so that it repels water and dirt.

## Taking Care of Vinyl

Vinyl has been around since World War II. All of us are familiar with the products needed to clean and polish vinyl in the home: vinyl floors, vinyl porch furniture, and PVC house siding. Fortunately, vinyl has found its way into boats in fenders, headliners, cushions, lifeline chafe protectors, and many other applications. Most of the vinyl cleaners and polishes you use at home work equally well on the boat. Try to avoid abrasive cleaners that will dull almost any vinyl finish. Be careful when using insect spray around vinyl as the spray's solvents (such as acetone or lacquer thinner) may soften or dissolve the plastic. Here are cleaning and maintenance tips for specific vinyl products on your boat:

### DODGER WINDOWS

Vinyl windows are delicate and easily marred. They're also quickly degraded by ultraviolet (UV) light, easily scratched, and prone to cracking. Vinyl is not the easiest plastic to maintain. The secret is to protect the clear vinyl with a coating that will prevent scratching and offer some protection against UV light.

Avoid abrasive cleaners and those containing alcohol. The best approach is to use a product like STAR BRITE PLASTIC POLISH/RESTORER, which fills in all the fine scratches. It can't be expected to work as well on badly marred surfaces. Use a soft cloth. Paper towels will scratch vinyl.

Storing vinyl without creating creases is difficult. Easily said, but hard to do, is to store flexible vinyl in a way that will minimize sharp bends and creases. Rolling up flexible vinyl carelessly will cause scratches and cuts, or distort the plastic's clear optical quality. There are no tricks to doing this, other than to pay careful attention as you roll up the window.

### FENDERS

White sidewall tire cleaner, available at automotive stores, does a good job of cleaning vinyl fenders. If that doesn't do it, try CASTROL SUPER CLEAN. If the plastic is still too dirty, clean it the best you can, then spray-paint it white. For tar stains on fenders and topsides, try applying WD-40. Automotive stores sell tar removers that also work. Use the solvent xylol on fenders as a last ditch effort. Let it sit on the fender for five minutes, then wipe off and rinse thoroughly.

### HEADLINERS

Vinyl headliners are often embossed like corduroy for an aesthetic effect, but this makes a surface that is difficult to clean. Scrub it with a stiff-bristled brush and FANTASTIK. Wipe it dry with a terry-cloth towel. The towel's rough texture will get into most of the embossed recesses and wipe away the loosened dirt.

### CUSHIONS

FANTASTIK and many other no-rinse, household spray cleaners remove most common stains from vinyl-covered cushions with a wipe. The beautiful part is that no rinsing is required. You can use alcohol to remove ink stains from vinyl cushions, but be sure to rinse it off afterward. To remove mildew from cushions, clean them with mild detergent. If they are severely mildewed, carefully add ammonia and hydrogen peroxide to the water, and scrub them.

Cushions wet with salt water take forever to dry. Wipe them with freshwater to remove the salt. Prop the cushions upright in the sun and wind, and let nature finish the job.

### LIFELINE COVERS

Try cleaning vinyl lifeline cover tubes before replacing them. Rub the vinyl tube with a rag soaked with SOFT SCRUB WITH BLEACH. It is readily available at supermarkets. The cleaner contains bleach, which will aid in whitening the tubing. Rinse it off with freshwater and a rag. Don't try to clean it with kerosene, as is sometimes suggested. Kerosene will smear the grime instead of removing it.

After a season or two, vinyl lifeline cover tubes get brittle and crack. Peel off the dry spaghetti-like residue with pliers, but first cover the deck. When I did it, the pieces rained down like uncooked rice. Wipe the wire with WD-40 to counteract any rust, and snap on split vinyl tube replacements. They are inexpensive and easy to install.

## Caring for Line

Today, most rope is made of plastic: nylon, Dacron, or polypropylene. These plastics are often combined with exotic synthetic fibers such as Kevlar. Hemp and cotton rope are rarely seen today, as they are weaker and less resistant to weathering than the synthetics are.

Most rope manufacturers recommend an occasional freshwater wash of line that has been exposed to salt water. It isn't bad practice to allow the line to dry before storing it away. If you need to wash some line, put it in a tub, rinse it with freshwater and fabric cleaner, then dry it and store it. Don't use bleach, as it may weaken and discolor synthetic line. Only if the line is extremely dirty should you machine-wash it with mild detergent. Rinse it thoroughly. Rope manufacturers advise that strong detergents will remove the finish and degrade the strength of the line. Dry a clean wet line by loosely flaking it over the boat's lifeline or a clothesline.

To cut a line properly, wrap masking tape around the line at the proper spot. Make the cut at the midpoint of the tape. The cut ends won't fray, and there will be a sharp edge for whipping or heat sealing. Seal frayed rope ends by touching the fibers with the flame of a butane lighter, a match, or a hot knife. Wrap whipping thread tightly for about a half-inch on each end of the line as an additional measure to prevent unraveling.

Rotate lines end-for-end to change the wear spots.

## Protect Your Topsides

Save the boat's fiberglass gelcoat from being damaged when vinyl fenders rub against the topsides. If you can, moor the boat in the middle of the slip, so that the fenders don't rub. If you slip terry-cloth covers over your fenders, you will have little or no damage from the fender at those unavoidable times when they rub against the hull.

## Replacing a Halyard

If a halyard has broken, or if its end has run over the sheave at the masthead, you will have to replace it. Go to the top of the mast in a bosun's chair. Drop a steel nut attached to fishing line down through the mast. Have your partner open the mast-bottom access plate, and attract the steel nut with a magnet on a stick. Your partner can then attach the new halyard to the fishing line. From the masthead, you can pull the halyard up through the mast and over the sheave again.

To replace an existing halyard, it's easier to use the old one as a "messenger." Create a temporary splice between the old line and the new, then use the old halyard to pull the new line safely up and over the masthead sheave. To make a temporary splice, butt the end of the old halyard against an end of the new halyard. Place at least six inches of duct tape lengthwise along the line where the rope-ends touch, and press it firmly against the line. Make the joint as smooth as possible because it will have to pass through the narrow sheave housing.

I have used sail twine to stitch the two lines together end-to-end as a further precaution against parting. Test the connection by giving a good pull on the joined line. Now, using the old halyard, pull the new line through the sheave and down to the deck. Measure the bitter end so that it reaches the waterline with enough spare to cleat it at the mast. The extra length to the waterline may come in handy some day when you want to use the halyard to rescue a person overboard.

Make a point of lying back occasionally and scanning the running rigging with binoculars. If a problem is developing aloft, you'll catch it early.

# Boat Hoses

Marine-grade hoses are used all over the boat and must be kept in first-class condition as they are a key ingredient of safety. The construction of the hose will determine its suitability for a specific use. For each application, there is a special hose, but sometimes the choices are confusing.

- Sanitation hose should be smooth inside, flexible, and odor-resistant. Rubber or vinyl hoses are usually stipulated for sanitation use.

- Freshwater hoses must be FDA-approved for use with drinking water. Reinforced potable-water hose is used for pressurized systems. Heavy-duty, reinforced rubber potable-water hose will be necessary for hot-water systems. Hoses for filling and venting tanks must be of the special, heavy-duty sanitation/water hose type.

- Bilge-discharge hose is made of ribbed polyethylene, vinyl, or rubber.

- Raw-water intake, engine coolant, and drainage hoses must be resistant to heat, kinking, and antifreeze solutions. They must also be suitable for below-the-waterline applications.

- Exhaust hose is made of silicone or rubber. It must be tolerant of enormous changes in temperature.

- Fuel hose is heavy-walled and reinforced for excellent flexibility. Type A1 is highly recommended.

With all these choices, you'll need to be very careful to use the correct hose when making a replacement. Using hose with a smooth interior is recommended in almost all situations. Use two hose clamps on any through-hull fitting below the waterline. Be sure both clamps are placed so they grip the barb. The clamping load will be distributed better if you don't align the clamps identically. When in doubt, double-clamp. Check the clamps on a regular basis for rust and loose screws. Be certain that a sharp edge has not begun to cut into the hose.

## Water Hose

Several problems plague water hoses on boats, ranging from plant growth to freezing in winter. Here are some ways to tackle individual problems.

### ELIMINATING ALGAE

Algae grows easily in clear plastic tubing. To reduce the frequency of cleaning, replace the clear tubing with opaque hose. Because light does not penetrate opaque tubing, algae will not grow as easily. Many manufacturers of new boats now prefer opaque, rigid PVC pipe for freshwater systems. The

Whale company, which manufactures many kinds of pumps for boats, has been using this approach for some time now.

### CLEANING WATER HOSE

When you need to clean the inside of tubing, dip a Q-TIP in CLOROX and attach it to a long piece of wire, then pull it through the hose. Clean the exterior of the hose with water and white vinegar, or with WINDEX.

### SMELLY HOSES

Sea water left to stand in a hose will eventually acquire a sulfurous odor caused by bacteria growth. Close the through-hull connections, and pump a solution of diluted bleach, or a cup of white vinegar, through the hose and leave it overnight. After you open the seacock, rinse the lines with plain water.

If nothing gets rid of the odor, wrap the hose in saran wrap designed to be impermeable to odors. It will improve the atmosphere considerably until you have the opportunity to install new water hose.

### WINTERIZE FOR LESS

Hardware stores sell insulation that can be wrapped around an exterior water hose. For liveaboards, it does an excellent job of keeping the hose from freezing solid in winter weather. If you allow a slow drip of water to run out of an outdoor hose, it will help keep the hose from freezing in all but the most extreme weather.

### BILGE DISCHARGE

To keep bilge discharge away from the topsides, jam a three-inch piece of clear water hose into the bilge pump outflow hole in the boat's topsides, so that it sticks out a few inches. This short piece of unobtrusive hose will shoot the bilge discharge clear of the boat and prevent ugly bilge stains from marring the topsides.

## Fuel Hose

It is well known that a faulty fuel or exhaust hose can be extremely dangerous. While there is no simple answer to maintaining fuel or exhaust hose, constant inspection, keeping a clean engine, routing hoses clear of the hot engine, checking the hose clamps, feeling the hoses for stickiness, and looking for leaks and wear are essential.

On gasoline fuel lines, wipe the hose with a clean rag and check for the smell of gasoline. When replacement is dictated, the best-quality hose should be your choice. For gasoline, A1-graded fuel hose is the top of the line, and well worth the extra price. These are not items were economy should prevail.

For exhaust hose, it is highly recommended that you consider a silicone hose, like Trident, which lasts up to six times as long as less expensive rubber hose.

### Double clamping

Fuel hose is another application where double-clamping is essential to safe boating. Fuel, particularly highly flammable gasoline, must not be allowed to leak due to the potential for explosion or fire.

### Use your nose

Even with all the fancy fume detectors on the market, don't underestimate your own sense of smell. If the odor of fuel, hot oil, or hot rubber is noticeable, immediately start looking for the source of the smell. It's possible that a hose has shaken loose somewhere. A good nose can often detect an unusual smell that sophisticated equipment might miss.

# Quick-Reference Guide
## Plastic, Vinyl, Line, and Rubber

| MATERIAL | TOPIC | JOB | PAGE | PRODUCT | HOW TO DO JOB |
|---|---|---|---|---|---|
| **Plastic** | Rigid plastic | Cleaning | 114 | **WINDEX**; white vinegar | Spray onto plastic. Wipe with cloth not paper |
| | | Removing minor scratches | 114 | **STAR BRITE PREMIUM MARINE POLISH WITH TEFLON** | Clean plastic. Apply polish. Buff with cloth. |
| | | Removing serious scratch | 114–115 | **BRASSO**; **NOXON 7**; **MICROMESH** | Test first. Buff carefully with **BRASSO** or **NOXON 7**. **MICROMESH** if all else fails. |
| | | Repel water | 115 | **RAIN X** | Clean. Apply **RAIN X** to make glass or plastic water-repellent. |
| **Vinyl** | | Cleaning roll-up windows | 115 | **STAR BRITE PLASTIC POLISH/ RESTORER** | Carefully apply polish to vinyl with a soft cloth. |
| | Fenders | Dirty | 116 | Sidewall cleaner; **CASTROL SUPER CLEAN** | Wipe on automotive sidewall cleaner or **CASTROL**. Follow directions to clean. |
| | | Tar | 116 | **WD-40 SPRAY LUBRICANT**; tar remover; xylol | Spray on **WD-40** or apply auto tar remover. Wipe off. xylol as a last resort |
| | Headliners | Dirty | 116 | **FANTASTIK** | Scrub using **FANTASTIK**, wipe with terry cloth towel |
| | Cushions | Dirty | 116 | **FANTASTIK** | Scrub with **FANTASTIK**. |
| | | Ink stain | 116 | Alcohol | Wipe alcohol on, rinse with water. |
| | | Mildew | 116 | Ammonia | Clean with mild detergent, wipe with ammonia. |
| | | Salt-water soaked. | 116 | Water | Rinse salt away with freshwater. Dry in the sun. |

*continues*

Quick-Reference Guide

**Quick-Reference Guide**

## Quick-Reference Guide
### Plastic, Vinyl, Line, and Rubber (continued)

| MATERIAL | TOPIC | JOB | PAGE | PRODUCT | HOW TO DO JOB |
|---|---|---|---|---|---|
| **Vinyl, ctd.** | Lifeline covers | Dirty | 116 | **SOFT SCRUB WITH BLEACH** | Rub covers with **SOFT SCRUB WITH BLEACH**. Rinse with water. |
| | Wire covers | Rusty | 116 | **CLOROX; WD-40 SPRAY LUBRICANT** | Rub wire with detergent, then **CLOROX**. Wipe with **WD-40**. |
| **Rope** | | Dirty | 117 | Water | Wash. Flake out to dry in sun. |
| **Hose** | Water hose | Eliminating algae | 118 | PVC pipe | Replace clear freshwater hose with opaque hose. Try rigid PVC pipe. |
| | | Cleaning | 119 | Bleach; **WINDEX** | Pull a bleach-soaked swab through hose. Clean exterior with **WINDEX**. |
| | | Removing smells | 119 | White vinegar; bleach | Close seawater intake. Put small amount of vinegar or bleach in hose. Rinse. |

# INTERIOR MAINTENANCE

In this chapter, I discuss cleaning and maintaining hard surfaces in the cabin, such as sinks, the icebox, freshwater tanks, and the bilge. At the end of the chapter, you'll find a section on maintaining electric and electronic components. The cleaning and maintenance of soft interior surfaces like upholstery, carpet, clothing, and headliners are discussed in chapters 7 and 8.

Inside the boat, away from the destructive elements of sun, rain, salt, and pollution, there is a different set of problems to deal with—mildew, odors, dust, and dirt. Most of the interior hard surfaces on modern recreational boats are made of wood, fiberglass, plastic, or metal. They're the same materials that are used outside, but they're less susceptible to wear and damage. Many of my recommendations involve hard-surface household cleaners. Go easy on the use of cleaners in the cabin. Use them as judiciously as you would at home.

## General Cleaning Tips

You'll make your life much easier if you keep all your cleaning supplies together. Stow the most frequently used cleaning materials like rags, scrubbing pads, and brushes in a bucket. When you're ready to use them, you won't need to start searching for them individually.

### ONE STEP AT A TIME

One way to stay ahead of what may seem the least desirable job on the boat, cleaning, is to work thoroughly on a small area each week. Tackle only one project at a time: the head, the galley, or the V-berth. Don't forget to dig into drawers, lockers, and lazarettes. The out-of-sight-out-of-mind syndrome is why mildew was invented.

## Avoiding Cabin Fever

Use color to bring the interior to life. Decorate the cabin settees with contrasting color pillows. Hang swinging wire baskets of fruit—but stow them when you go to sea, of course. Add a new tone to the boat with the subtle sound of wind chimes.

CONDENSATION

Absorb the humidity always present in closed spaces on the boat with an open box of cat litter or a bag of charcoal briquettes. **MDR DAMP AWAY** containers collect up to 17 times their weight in water. The chemical can be dried in a conventional oven and used again.

When temperatures differ inside and outside the boat, sweating of the interior surfaces of the hull and lockers is an inevitable result. This winter condition plagues liveaboards. Slit open a bag of cat litter, silica absorbent, or charcoal briquettes and place some in an unobtrusive place near the sweating problem to soak up the moisture. Under severe conditions, there is never enough absorbent to stop the sweating. Wiping the walls down frequently with towels will give some temporary relief. Opening hatches will equalize the humidity but let in unwanted cold air. The only real help is to

# An Expert's View

**Keith Irwing** is an anomaly among the experts I interviewed for the book. He is a true innovator, a person willing to try new ideas. His hands-on, practical methods encourage the use of maintenance products more often used in the home and on automobiles. His earlier years were spent as a car mechanic until he found a 28-foot, 1969 Chris-Craft and switched his allegiance to boat-engine maintenance. When I asked what other boats he had owned, he shook his head and said, "Too many to remember."

Powerboats went by the wayside when he met his bride-to-be on her 42-foot Hunter sailboat. They moved on to a 58-foot, German-built ferroconcrete boat, and now own a 48-foot CT ketch made in China in 1979.

He was rebedding exquisitely hand-carved cabin windows while we talked. I asked if we could discuss boat interiors and the maintenance of engines. True to form, his suggestions were right off the cleaner shelf at the supermarket.

"Let's start up here," he said pointing to his brightwork. "I pretty much stick to ammonia cleaners in the cabin but when I really want to clean wood that hasn't had a lot of care for years, I use a combination of **CASTROL SUPER CLEAN** and trisodium phosphate (TSP). This is powerful stuff and will clean anything. Most automobile supply stores have **CASTROL SUPER CLEAN**. To keep my brightwork clean, I use diluted **CASTROL SUPER CLEAN** and bleach. To clean interior woodwork, I use either **MURPHY'S OIL SOAP SPRAY** if it needs a simple cleaning, or **OLD ENGLISH GOLD** to polish finished wood to bring out a good furniture look."

open the lockers and cabinets and use fans to provide considerable interior air circulation.

## VACUUMING

Most boats have innumerable places that are completely out of reach, where dust and debris maliciously settle. Purchase a small wet-and-dry vacuum cleaner with at least a 2.5-hp motor. Using duct tape, attach a foot-long piece of quarter-inch flexible plastic tubing to the suction end of the hose. Now you have a small tube that can reach into places where the vacuum's thin wand won't go.

Another approach is to buy one of the miniature air sprays sold at computer stores. A quick blast of air can blow dirt out of some extremely tight places.

He walked over to the sink. "To keep my sinks from having the bad smell that comes from water sitting in the hoses, I use a biodegradable freshwater treatment, either STAR BRITE WATER CONDITIONER or PURICLEAN. Just a little bit keeps the water from getting a bad odor and won't dry out the hoses as bleach will do. While we're talking about water storage, there's a good way to clean out your water tanks and holding tanks. Feed a stiff, ⅜-inch hose down the feed tube to the bottom of the tank. It will follow most reasonable bends in the line. Pump water into the tank. The flow at the bottom of the tank will agitate any sediment, which can then be pumped out more easily.

"The bilge is another story. All bilges are different. Access on some is difficult. I can easily get to mine and just spray some biodegradable CASTROL SUPER CLEAN into the bilge and hose it down well then pump it out.

"A clean engine doesn't seem important, but if it's clean you can see problems. Leaks become obvious. Cleaning an engine is easy. With the engine off, I cover the air intake or carburetor, belts and alternator, then spray CASTROL SUPER CLEAN all over the engine. After a minute, I hose it down with fresh water. When it's dry, I do paint touch-ups if necessary, then spray CRC CORROSION INHIBITOR or WD-40 everywhere. Remember to start up the engine to burn off any excess CRC or WD-40. I do this quite often when I winterize boats.

"Preventive maintenance is the only answer to keeping an engine problem-free. It's really just common sense. Keep your eyes and ears tuned to changes in the way things look and sound. Check the oil before you start the engine. Touch all the hose clamps with a screwdriver to see if they are loose. Check the bilge pump float by flipping it with your hand to be sure it's not stuck. These are just a few of the things to be checked before startup.

"Keep spare parts on the boat. Something will break where and when you least expect it. Every year, I get a fresh tube of RTV SILICONE GASKET COMPOUND. You can make a gasket of any size or shape in minutes. Have two, not one, water-pump repair kits on the boat. If you've picked up something and the problem occurs again, the extra kit will give you the redundancy you need. It goes without saying to keep extra oil filters, enough oil for a full replacement, and each size of engine belt. There's really nothing to it," he said smiling.

Home Depot sells a similar, air-blast product for about $10. It can be considered a throwaway for the really messy jobs.

### SMALL SURFACES

FANTASTIK works well on almost all small surfaces. Its best claim to fame is that, when used indoors, it doesn't need to be rinsed. Outside, any alkaline cleaner should be rinsed and not allowed to dry.

### WALLS AND FLOORS

MURPHY'S OIL SOAP diluted in a bucket of water is a household floor-cleaning standard. Now, the company has come out with an easier-to-use version in a spray bottle, which, when spritzed onto wood surfaces, cleans and polishes without the need for rinsing. It's compact and leaves wood in terrific condition.

### INTERIOR WOOD

PLEDGE is another household wood-polishing product found in almost every kitchen. It's easy to use and keeps the boat's interior wood in first-class shape.

### PICKING UP DUST

Try spraying ENDUST on a clean paintbrush to pick up dust. Just paint the corners with the treated brush to get dust and dirt out of the crevices. Slip your hand into an old sock that has been sprayed with ENDUST, and you'll find it works better in tight spots than a plain dust rag does.

## Toilets and Sinks

It's important to keep heads and sinks spotlessly clean, not only for purposes of hygiene, but also as an aid to maintenance. On many boats, both the galley and the head have hoses containing salt water, which, left to its own devices, will develop a vile smell that permeates the whole boat.

### Heads

Marine toilets must comply with local and federal regulations that are rapidly becoming more restrictive. Most boats of cruising size are equipped with holding tanks that are periodically pumped out at a marina discharge station. Sanitation chemicals are used to maintain a clean, odor-free environment on the boat.

On the exterior of the toilet, it's a fairly simple job to keep the bowl clean. A household cleaner such as FANTASTIK will do a good job of cleaning the *exterior* porcelain and plastic surfaces of the head.

STAR BRITE TOILET BOWL CLEANER/LUBRICANT squirted into the bowl removes stains without scrubbing. Most domestic toilet cleaners are too harsh for boat use and can damage the valves in the pumping mechanism. Don't use them in a marine toilet. The toilet can be freshened occasionally with a dose of white vinegar or baking soda.

You won't have to use a toilet-bowl cleaner very often if the toilet is pumped out thoroughly after each use, occasionally lubricated with WEST MARINE HEAD LUBE and rinsed with white vinegar.

There are dozens of toilet and holding-tank deodorants on the market. Most are biodegradable and no longer contain formaldehyde as they once did. Many of them contain chemicals that break down waste. THETFORD'S AQUA-KEM HOLDING TANK DEODORANT and MDR HEAD ZYME are two popular brands.

WEST MARINE HEAD LUBE is excellent at keeping head valves working easily. Mineral oil does a good job but is only effective for a short period. When you find that lubrication becomes a frequent chore, it's probably time to get a toilet rebuild kit.

A good way to determine if your toilet output hose is allowing odor to escape is to wipe the hose with a cloth and smell it for odor (to deal with bad odors, see Boat Hoses in chapter 8).

## Bug-Free Fuel

BIOBOR JF is a microbiocide used to eliminate and prevent the growth of certain organisms in diesel fuel. Each fall, the boatowner has the option of draining the fuel tank completely, or filling it to the top, with the object of preventing water condensation in the tank during the winter lay-up.

Those boaters who prefer a full tank will normally add a biocide to keep "bugs" from growing in the fuel. BIOBOR JF is soluble in fuel and water, and is designed to migrate from the fuel phase to the water phase for complete control of fungus.

The directions call for very specific amounts to be added to an exact quantity of diesel fuel. This amount is easily measured from the dispenser and added to the fuel inlet as you fill the tank. MDR STOR-N-START contains additives that act as a gasoline stabilizer by protecting and keeping it fresh during storage.

## Sinks

Stainless-steel sinks can be maintained indefinitely with a soft-powder cleaner like BON AMI or BAR KEEPERS FRIEND. If stains persist, use bronze wool with a soft cleanser like BON AMI. Wipe a stainless sink with a paper towel after use. Water stains and spots don't appear on a dry sink.

Clean out clogged drains by using the rubber top of a kitchen basting syringe. Insert it into the sink drain and squeeze it. Like a plumber's helper, it will break up simple pipe obstructions.

As we've already seen, salt water sitting in the input hose will develop a sulfurous smell if the sink is not used frequently. There is no smell quite as bad as the one that occurs when you turn on the water spigot after not using it for weeks. You can eliminate most odors coming out of the galley-sink drain by flushing it with white vinegar at the end of each trip. In some instances, replacing an old input hose is the only way to get rid of unwanted smells. Old hose gets pitted on the inside, allowing algae and bacteria to find a home. New hose has a smooth interior and is less likely to cause odors.

# The Galley

## CLEANING DISHES

Wipe dirty dishes with a paper towel to remove any remaining food. Rinse the dishes with a small amount of water. Scrub them, using a drop of JOY. Most boaters use JOY because it is almost the only detergent that will foam in cold salt water. Rinse with freshwater and put the dishes in a drying rack fitted into a big oven roasting pan or an aluminum turkey tray. The dripping water will end up in the tray and not on the counter.

An easy method for cleaning extremely dirty pots and pans is to put some detergent and water into the soiled pot and place it on the stove. Boil it for a few minutes. Any burned-on residue can now be scraped away easily.

When you're cooking pasta, rinse the strainer as soon as you remove the pasta, or the starch will stick like glue when it dries, and be much harder to remove.

Incidentally, why not use paper plates and cups to avoid cleaning dishes altogether?

## CONSERVING DISHWASHING WATER

At home, some people wash one dish at a time with the water faucet running constantly. On a cruise, however, freshwater is precious. Wipe the food off dishes with paper towels, as previously suggested. Wet all the dishes with water. With the water faucet turned off, soap the dishes. Rinse, then place them on a terry-cloth towel to dry. Using this technique will cut water usage by 90 percent.

## Galley Grease Fires

A scrupulously clean galley will prevent the build-up of grease, which is a frequent cause of shipboard fires. If you should be unlucky enough to experience a grease fire, don't throw water on it—you'll just scatter the flames around. A grease fire is classified as a Class B fire, so be sure your extinguishers are capable of handling that classification. They usually contain dry chemical powders or carbon dioxide. In an emergency, you can also use baking soda, salt, flour, or sand to smother a grease fire.

Incidentally, don't rely on fire extinguisher gauges as a guarantee that the charge is still in the green. Gauges fail all too often. Have the unit weighed annually to determine if the extinguisher is fully charged. Occasionally, remove the extinguisher from its bracket, turn it upside down and shake it to loosen any dry chemical that has settled to the bottom. Replace all extinguishers every few years. They are inexpensive, and knowing they are new gives you great peace of mind. Have a practice fire-drill with an out-of-date extinguisher.

### CLEANING THE ICEBOX

No matter how meticulous you are, food particles will lodge in the farthest recesses of the icebox. Liquids will attach themselves to the sides. Unwanted odors will arrive overnight. Only forgotten garbage can equal the odor of a dirty icebox that, when opened, fouls the entire boat. Empty the icebox regularly, and clean it with ammonia, bleach, or WINDEX.

Baking soda has been used for years as an extremely effective cleaner and deodorizer. Wipe the icebox interior with a solution of baking soda and water. Pour the mixture down the sink when you're done. It's good for the pipes. Put an open baking-soda box in the icebox where it will continue its job and absorb unwanted odors.

Leave the door or the lid of the icebox open when you are off the boat. Once again, fresh air prevents most odor and mildew problems.

# Freshwater Tanks

At spring commissioning, you will probably want to clean your freshwater tank. Flush the tank, then add a pint of CLOROX to a half-filled tank. Agitate the water if possible. Flush it several times to remove the chlorine taste from the water. When you fill it, you should have good-tasting water once more.

Marine stores sell water-purifying and taste-improving tablets that can be dropped into the inlet when you are filling the water tanks. They taste better than bleach. Try keeping your water fresh with AQUA TABS, tasteless tablets that kill bacteria and algae when dropped into the tank. A more elaborate plan is to install a water filtration unit. The Culligan company sells an under-sink drinking-water filter unit at marine stores. When you connect it to the freshwater input hose, it filters out foreign particles and most odors.

# Bilges

A clean bilge is not just a good idea from the standpoint of odor and cleanliness but from a safety standpoint as well. Hair, paint chips, paper, and other debris can clog limber holes and pump strainers to the point where boat safety is at risk. Keeping the bilge clean and well maintained is therefore an issue of safety as well as cleanliness.

## *Cleaning*

As a first choice, you may wish to use an environmentally acceptable conventional cleaner that can work well if the bilge is thoroughly rinsed and pumped out afterwards. Comparison tests by *Practical Sailor* magazine rated MEAN GREEN BOAT AND RV CLEANER a top choice for cleaning bilges.

SUDBURY BILGE CLEANER and BOATLIFE BILGE CLEANER are both biodegradable bilge cleaners that will deodorize and dissolve grease and oil. They are put into the bilge and allowed to slosh around until the bilge is clean and pumped out. A small quantity may be left in bilges with areas you cannot reach or empty.

An industrial degreaser called ULTRA SOLV is sold by commercial janitorial supply houses and you can use it as a high-powered yet inexpensive bilge cleaner. It contains phosphates, and it can harm aluminum, but it works very well. Clean up ULTRA SOLV responsibly by removing the liquid and depositing it in a marina disposal station.

Once the bilge is dry, remove any oily residue with trisodium phosphate (TSP) cleaner. Keep TSP away from aluminum as well. TSP is a phosphate product, so dispose of it responsibly at a marina disposal station.

For picking up oil from the bilge, diapers are the most absorbent materials you can economically purchase. Store a box on board and use them to sponge up the oil-water grime in the bilge and under the engine. One product that seems to do the job of removing aromas from bilges and holding tanks is MICROBE-CLEAN MARINE, from the Georgetown Environmental Group, of Washington, D.C. They appear to have found the right bacteria content to eat up the petroleum and waste that causes noxious odors in boat bilges.

## Coatings

Although the aesthetic payoff is minimal, painting the bilge is a good idea. Cracks in the bilge fiberglass will allow water to seep into the laminate. The right coating will seal the cracks and keep water out of the fiberglass. A painted bilge also presents a smooth surface for cleaning. Bilge water often offers the first sign of an oil or fuel leak. A white background enamel makes it far easier to see.

Remove all debris that has collected in the bilge. Clean the bilge thoroughly with a solvent cleaner to remove oil and grease. If additional cleaning is needed, wipe down with a TSP solution and rinse. Dry thoroughly. Apply two coats of a bilge paint such as INTERLUX BILGEKOTE 863, a high-gloss, light-gray enamel formulated to prevent absorption of oil, gasoline, and other gray-water contaminants by fiberglass or wood hulls. Two-part RUSTOLEUM EPOXY CONCRETE SURFACER, available at hardware stores, will also do an excellent job.

# Bugs and Vermin

After a winter lay-up, you might be concerned about the possibility that insects will hatch on board your boat in the first warm weather. The last thing you want is a swarm of insects on the first cruise of the season. Set off a bug-bomb a few days before re-commissioning to give yourself peace of mind.

Camping stores have bugproof mosquito nets that set up in minutes. Rig one of these enclosures over a bunk to protect yourself from biting insects. Purchasing replacement screens for the numerous ports and hatches on the boat is often difficult if not impossible. Make your own screens using one of the following ideas.

You can attach plastic window screening to ports and hatches with VELCRO. Home Depot sells screen kits with aluminum frames, plastic corners, and fiberglass window screening. I rounded the plastic corner pieces on a grinding wheel, so they fit my hatch. To make

## Insect Bites

I've found that cornstarch, white vinegar, and baking soda all help soothe insect bites. Ammonia will take the itch out of mosquito bites. It is also advisable to keep an emergency bee-sting kit on board.

a screen that will fit an unusually shaped hatch perfectly, try this idea. Lay a piece of brown paper or stiff paper over the hatch or port opening. Carefully cut the paper with a sharp knife or razor blade, following the exact contours of where you want the screen to rest. Use the paper template to transfer the screen's outer dimensions to a piece of thin FORMICA plastic laminate. Make two identical pieces from the paper template. Cut a hole in the center of each piece of the plastic laminate, about a half-inch in from the outer edge. You now have two frames to place the screen material between.

Apply a marine sealant like BOATLIFE LIFE SEAL around the perimeter of the FORMICA pieces and assemble them as a sandwich with the screen in the middle. Place weights on the frame while the sealant cures. Trim the excess screen material as close as possible until you get a smooth edge. You now have a custom-sized, rigid screen to place in the hatch or port window.

My East Coast marina is infested with carpenter bees that I, at first, thought were bumblebees. Local boatowners say that carpenter bees search for unpainted wood and can, in no time, bore a perfect 3/16-inch hole deep into the wood.

Some marinas in the upper Chesapeake Bay are infested with spiders. I hate to destroy spiders, as they supposedly feast on the more bothersome flying insects, but their excrement is all but impossible to remove from the deck. CASTROL SUPER CLEAN at full strength removes fresh spider stains quite easily. Wear protective gloves, and rinse the deck thoroughly when you have finished spot-cleaning.

In the tropics, boaters try to avoid bringing supplies on board in corrugated boxes or brown paper bags. Cockroaches use them as transportation from stores to the boat. Boric acid in bottle caps will get rid of these pesky pests. If you can find it at your supermarket, 20 MULE TEAM BORAX works well as a cockroach deterrent and also does a good job of ridding the boat of ants.

Mosquito coils and citronella are old fashioned but are still popular and effective repellents. AVON'S SKIN-SO-SOFT moisturizer seems to keep tiny no-see-um pests at bay.

# Maintaining Electric and Electronic Components

## Electrical Systems

Only marine wire and cable should be used on a boat, as each strand is tinned for corrosion resistance. Hardware-store wire intended for household use will corrode in a marine environment. When using a crimping tool to attach terminals to the wire, always double-crimp. You'll get a superior connection if you make two adjoining crimps rather than one.

Try to keep wires up and out of the bilge area if at all possible. Spray electric connections with **WD-40** to displace moisture and protect metal contacts. CRC HEAVY DUTY CORROSION INHIBITOR and BOESHIELD T-9 are two other good multi-purpose moisture displacers and lubricants. Petroleum jelly, while messy, is an effective lubricant and anticorrosion agent when used in moderate temperature connections. It will melt and flow off its intended location at high temperatures.

The damp, salt-air environment on a boat may cause light-bulb bases to corrode in the socket. Protect the bulb by rubbing a light coating of petroleum jelly on its base before inserting it into the light socket. A light coating will not impede electrical flow and will help prevent corrosion in the socket.

### BATTERY CARE

Don't mix gel-cell and lead-acid batteries. Use only one type or the other. Put batteries in battery boxes and strap them down to prevent their shifting in heavy weather. If the battery is warm to the touch, it's getting too hot. Overcharging probably causes this excess heat. Check to be sure your voltage regulator and battery charger are operating correctly. Wear chemical-resistant gloves and protective glasses whenever you work around batteries. Batteries contain sulfuric acid, which can splatter on your skin or eyes as you work on them.

To take the gunk and scale off the tops of batteries, remove the plastic terminal caps and brush away any corrosion. Using a wrench, disconnect the positive side of the battery first, then the negative side. Rotate a terminal cleaning tool on each terminal, then wire-brush the inside of the terminal ends. An old paintbrush can sweep away dirt and debris on the battery case. Clean the battery tops and sides with a combination of ammonia, weak detergent, and water. Then rinse off. If the plates inside deep cell batteries are exposed, fill each cell with enough distilled water to cover the plates.

When you reconnect the battery, place doughnut-shaped, chemically treated felt washers under the cable ends to reduce the possibility of acid corrosion at the terminals. They are available at the marine store. When you replace the lugs, first connect the negative cable end to the terminal and tighten, then connect the positive cable. Remember, positive terminal first off, last on. Protect the cleaned terminals from future corrosion with a light spray of CRC Heavy Duty Corrosion Inhibitor. The spray turns into an film that remains flexible and prevents corrosion at this critical location.

Petroleum jelly does a great job of protecting the cable ends but when the battery heats up, it melts and can run down and become an insulator between the battery terminal and the cable end. Petroleum jelly can actually turn black when it gets this hot.

## Electronics

For better electrical contact, use a silicone spray on the ferrule, the mounting threads, and the connection between your VHF radio and its antenna. Be careful not to overspray onto the fiberglass nearby.

WD-40 sprayed on the electrical connections on the back side of each electronic instrument keeps moisture and the subsequent corrosion from deteriorating your signals.

## Quick-Reference Guide

### Interior Maintenance

| Topic | Job | Page | Product | How to Do Job |
|---|---|---|---|---|
| **Cabin** | Condensation | 124 | MDR Damp Away | Place absorbent containers where needed. Wipe down wet bulkheads. Use fans to circulate air. |
| | Cleaning | 126 | Fantastik; Murphy's Oil Soap | Spray on. No rinsing required. |
| | Polishing | 126 | Pledge | Spray on. Wipe wood surfaces with clean rag. |
| | Dusting | 126 | Endust | Spray Endust on paintbrush or old sock to clean in tight corners. |
| **Heads** | Exterior cleaning | 126 | Fantastik | Spray on. Wipe clean. |
| | Interior cleaning | 126–127 | White vinegar | Leave in bowl for 30 minutes. Flush. |
| | Freshener | 127 | White vinegar; baking soda | Apply. Pump out bowl. |

*continues*

## *Quick-Reference Guide*

## Interior Maintenance *(continued)*

| TOPIC | JOB | PAGE | PRODUCT | HOW TO DO JOB |
|---|---|---|---|---|
| **Heads, ctd.** | Lubrication | 127 | **WEST MARINE HEAD LUBE;** mineral oil | Pour few ounces into bowl. Pump a few strokes. Let sit overnight. |
| | Holding tank deodorants | 127 | **THETFORD'S AQUA-KEM HOLDING TANK DEODORANT; MDR HEAD ZYME** | Add specified amount to head. Pump into holding tank. |
| **Sinks** | Cleaning | 127 | **BON AMI; BAR KEEPERS FRIEND** | Sprinkle on wet sink. Rub with scrubbing pad. Rinse. |
| | Smelly | 127 | White vinegar | Flush smelly sink with white vinegar. |
| **Galley** | Cleaning grease | 128 | **FANTASTIK** | Wipe off grease from oven and under burners. Clean with **FANTASTIK.** |
| | Dishes | 128 | **JOY** | Wipe dishes. Rinse. Clean with **JOY**. Rinse in freshwater. |
| | Pots and pans | 128 | Detergent | Boil water and detergent in dirty pot. Scrape off residue. |
| | Ice-box odor | 129 | **WINDEX;** baking soda | Clean with **WINDEX** or baking soda. Leave box of baking soda in icebox. Leave door open when off boat. |
| **Freshwater tanks** | Cleaning | 129 | **CLOROX** | Add pint of **CLOROX** to half-filled tank. Agitate. Flush multiple times. |
| | Freshen | 129 | **AQUA-TABS** | Drop into tank. |
| **Bilges** | Cleaning | 129 | **MEAN GREEN BOAT AND RV CLEANER** | Place in bilge. Pump out after 24 hours. |
| | Degreaser | 129–130 | **ULTRA SOLV;** TSP; **SUDBURY BILGE CLEANER; BOATLIFE BILGE CLEANER** | Clean bilge with **ULTRA SOLV** for heavy cleaning. Remove residue with TSP. For regular care, use biodegradable Sudbury or BoatLIFE products. |
| | Oil pickup | 130 | Diapers | Sponge up oil with diapers. |

| TOPIC | JOB | PAGE | PRODUCT | HOW TO DO JOB |
|---|---|---|---|---|
| **Bilges, ctd.** | Smelly bilge | 130 | **MICROBE-CLEAN MARINE** | Add to bilge. Pump out after 24 hours. |
| | Painting | 130 | **RUSTOLEUM EPOXY CONCRETE SURFACER; INTERLUX BILGEKOTE 863** | Clean bilge. Remove all oil, scale, and debris. Wipe surface with a solvent. Apply paint. Ventilate well. |
| **Bugs and Vermin** | Insect bites | 131 | Cornstarch; vinegar; baking soda; ammonia | Application of these natural products will soothe insect bites. |
| | Spider marks on deck | 131 | **CASTROL SUPER CLEAN** | Wear gloves and apply **CASTROL SUPER CLEAN** to spot. Rinse. |
| | Removing cockroaches | 131 | **20 MULE TEAM BORAX** | Place borax in bottle caps and place in areas where cockroaches run. |
| | Removing ants | 131 | Boric acid | Place in small dish and place near ants. |
| | Mosquito repellent | 131 | Citronella | Burn citronella candles near you at night. |
| | No-see-ums repellent | 131 | **AVON SKIN-SO-SOFT** moisturizer | Apply to exposed skin to repel no-see-ums. |

# 1

# PERIODIC UPKEEP SCHEDULES

**Y**ou probably have your own way of doing everything on your boat, and no two boats are precisely the same. But large or small, power or sailboat, gas or diesel, live-aboard or occasional tripper, if you follow a simple maintenance system, upkeep becomes less of a chore. In this section, there are simple checklists that can easily be adapted to your particular circumstances. While the lists are generalized, they provide a starting point for creating individual maintenance schedules.

## Boat Records

I began to gather information by organizing a three-ring binder with sections on every aspect of my boat. If I need information on the height of my mast, where the waste seacock is located, or where to find spare engine parts, it is right there in the binder that I keep on board. It is set up in seven broad categories, then broken down by subject.

### MAINTENANCE SECTION

This is where I keep my personalized upkeep and maintenance schedule, a list of repair projects to be done, and a list of items I need to buy for the boat.

### STATISTICS SECTION

Here I store information on hundreds of measurements, such as the height of my mast from the waterline, engine replacement part numbers, or the size of PVC lifeline cable covers. I keep notes on socket sizes for specific engine bolts to save me the trial and error method of fumbling with wrong-sized sockets in a tight, dark space.

### Boat systems section

I keep hand-drawn schematics of my plumbing and electrical layouts, drawings that show the exact locations of all through-hulls, photographs of the boat on slings to show future yard workers where to place the straps, and a list of all the instruction manuals for the equipment on the boat. These manuals sometimes suggest maintenance intervals and methods of care. Look at them. They harbor a wealth of information. You might even want to go so far as to paint a schematic diagram on the underside of floor boards to detail the plumbing and electric layouts below in the bilge.

### Boat-paper section

This is where I keep copies, not the originals, of my documentation, registration, mortgage, bill of sale, and survey. There's also a page or two listing the names and addresses of commercial people and personal friends I have met along the way. Copies are expendable, originals are not. I no longer have to say to myself, "Where's that envelope scrap with the name of those people who had drinks with me in Cape May?"

### Boat inventory section

Here is where I list the location of everything I've stored in the dozen or so lockers, lazarettes, and under-bunk hideaways. This is the hardest list to keep accurate.

### Boat expenses section

Though I keep this information on my Excel computer program, I have a copy in the binder for quick reference. It allows me to look months ahead and see an upcoming expense. No surprises; that's the key to how I juggle my finite income. The spreadsheet covers subjects like monthly fuel costs, mortgage expense, docking-fee due dates, and supplies I've purchased.

### Ship's logs

In addition to my systems and maintenance book, I keep two logs. A trip log contains dates, weather conditions, destinations, distance traveled, and comments on each trip I take. I have a separate column for engine hours, oil changes, and part replacement dates. It helps to know how long it has been since the last refueling, or oil change, or impeller replacement. For fun, and to settle arguments at a later date, I ask my guests to write a short comment in a guest log book. It's great sport on a cold winter night, to read back over the summer's adventures.

## Maintenance Schedules

It may not be possible to follow any maintenance schedule exactly, but if you review these lists at each suggested time, you will be reminded of jobs that have to be done. Modify the lists for your own personal touch.

## Before You Go

Use this checklist before you leave the dock.

- Fuel tank full
- Water tank full
- Engine seacock open
- Check alternator belt tension
- Check oil level
- Ice on board
- Someone has been advised of destination and ETA
- Spare engine oil and parts on board
- Liferings are in their holders
- Check bilge
- Visually inspect standing rigging
- Disconnect shore power

## After Startup

Here's what to do after the engine is started.

- Check for proper oil pressure and temperature
- Check cooling-water temperature gauge
- Check that cooling water is flowing out of the exhaust properly
- Check fuel filter for contamination
- Check stuffing box drip
- Determine if batteries are charging
- Check if docking lines and fenders are on the boat
- Check that dinghy is securely tied to the boat, and not in the way, for departure

## Back Home

Run through this checklist after a day's cruise, when you're safely back at your mooring or in your slip.

- Battery switches on/off
- Top off fresh water
- Top off oil
- Top off fuel
- Check bilge
- Wash down deck with freshwater
- Chamois chrome and stainless deck fittings
- Store cushions and liferings below
- Clean anchor and tie it down

▶ Fenders out

▶ Covers on sails

▶ Icebox clean

▶ Portholes closed

▶ Wet clothing and towels removed

▶ Garbage ashore

▶ Dinghy put away

## Weekly Checks

Here are two things you should check every week, no matter what else you do.

▶ Check docking lines for chafe

▶ Check crankcase and reduction gear oil levels

## Every Month

These are jobs that need to be done once a month, every month.

▶ Open and close all seacocks. Determine ease of operation. Look for corrosion

▶ Scrub deck with soap and fresh water. Rinse thoroughly

▶ Wax chrome and stainless steel fittings

▶ Check varnish and retouch at the first sign of failure

▶ Check tightness of shrouds and lifelines

# Seasonal Tasks

There are two hectic seasons for many boaters: when the boat is hauled out for the winter, and when it's launched again in spring. If you're lucky enough to live in a warm climate, and are able to keep your boat in the water all year, some of the winterizing tasks mentioned below will not be necessary, and the others can be spread out over a longer period.

## Winter Schedule

Here's a list of jobs you'll need to do to keep your boat in good shape through the winter.

▶ Choose whether you will top off the engine fuel tank, or drain it. Close fuel shut-off valve

▶ Drain water from engine, or add antifreeze

▶ Close seacocks

▶ Remove cooling-water impeller so it doesn't take a set

▶ Drain or pump out warm crankcase oil and refill with fresh oil

▶ Take batteries ashore and maintain their charge over the winter

► Drain all pumps, hoses, and tanks

► Remove electronics from the boat to home storage

► Pump bilge dry

► Pump toilet dry and drain. Flood with marine lubricant if boat goes into dry storage

► Remove foul-weather gear, cushions, bedding, life jackets, sails, books, and provisions

► Remove anchor and store below

► Replace zincs below the waterline if you haul boat out

► Clean and lubricate winches and windlass

► Cover the boat if possible. Be sure there is ample ventilation

► Leave lockers and drawers open so they get air

► Wax everything for winter protection

► At home, work on small varnishing and repair jobs

► Have fire extinguishers recharged if necessary

► Check that bilge pump is fully operational if the boat stays in the water

► Treat toilet with antifreeze if you leave the boat in the water

► Place extra docking lines if boat remains in the water

► Put heavy-duty chafing gear on docking lines

► Keep notes on what has been winterized so there is no question when the process is reversed in the spring

► Review manuals for annual maintenance tasks

## Spring Schedule

Although you'll want to get your boat in the water quickly in the spring, it will pay you to take the time to go through this checklist. It may also pay you to start early, thus avoiding last-minute pressure from boatyards anxious to speed you into the water.

► Check zincs, rudder, propeller, propeller shaft, Cutless bearing, stuffing box, and through-hulls

► Reverse most winterizing procedures

► Clean and wax topsides again

► Haul and clean bottom if boat has been in the water all winter. Repaint if needed

► Check that cockpit drains are clear

► Check shroud and lifeline tension

► Check turnbuckles and rigging for tension and rust

► Inspect all electrical parts for loose connections and corrosion

► Check masthead electrical connections, fittings, pulleys, halyards, and roller-furling mechanism

- ▶ Clean interior, drains, and bilge
- ▶ Check ports and hatches for leaks that may have occurred over the winter
- ▶ Polish gelcoat, stainless steel, chrome, and Plexiglas
- ▶ Check chainplate condition
- ▶ Tighten all pertinent bolts and screws
- ▶ Check varnish for possible touch-up or refinishing
- ▶ Check steering
- ▶ Rinse and refill water tanks
- ▶ Refuel
- ▶ Check seacocks, hoses, clamps, belts, and tank fittings
- ▶ Check for oil stains and rust
- ▶ Install new filters. Change oil
- ▶ Reinstall or change impeller
- ▶ Check battery condition
- ▶ Test bilge pump and manual pumps
- ▶ Review manuals for annual maintenance jobs

# 2

# INDIVIDUAL MAINTENANCE TASKS

**T**his appendix contains an alphabetical list of a number of the possible cleaning and maintenance problems you'll encounter on your boat. The page numbers will guide you to the sections of the book where the solutions are discussed in detail.

Individual Maintenance Tasks

Individual Maintenance Tasks

# 3

# CLEANING AND
# MAINTENANCE
# PROJECTS

*T*his appendix lists specific sections of the boat, and the projects you'll need to carry out there. It is, in a way, a reminder that boats demand constant attention if they're to stay seaworthy and attractive. For example, if it strikes your fancy to work on deck on a sunny spring day, examine the pages listed under Deck. They'll suggest dozens of projects you might want to tackle while the good weather lasts.

Cleaning and Maintenance Projects

A3

Cleaning and Maintenance Projects

Cleaning and Maintenance Projects

# APPENDIX

# CHEMICAL INGREDIENTS

*T*his is a survey of the commercial products and common cleaning chemicals recommended in this book. Using the manufacturers' material safety data sheets (MSDS) and ingredients listed on labels, the active chemical components of these products have been identified. Brand-name products are listed under the chemical class of an active ingredient. If there is an important lesser ingredient, the product will also be listed in a second chemical class. For example, since Windex contains isopropanol alcohol and ammonia as active ingredients, it will be listed under both chemical categories. Should a boat-maintenance project such as serious gelcoat stain removal lend itself to the use of oxalic acid, this appendix will help you find products containing oxalic acid as an active ingredient.

Know the active ingredients in the compound you're using. If, for example, it contains oxalic acid or lye, you should always wear protective gloves and glasses. If it contains a solvent like acetone, you must be careful using it in a confined space or near an open flame from the stove. If it contains a known hazardous ingredient like chlorine, be sure to protect yourself from skin contact and inhalation of the fumes. In some cases, it may be wise to select a product less dangerous to your health. Use this index as a guide to protecting yourself from products that use hazardous chemicals to get the job done.

**1-Methyltriethylenedioxy (pesticide)**
Biobor JF

**Acetone**
3M Spray Trim Adhesive
Interlux Pintoff 299E

**Acrylic**
Armstrong's Floor Wax
Johnson's No Wax Floor Polish
New Glass

**Alcohol**
Windex

**Alkalate naphtha**
Sikkens Cetol Marine Finish

**Alkyd**
Interlux Bilgekote 863

**Aluminum hydroxide**
3M One Step Aluminum Restorer and
Polish
3M "One Step" Metal Restorer and Polish

**Aluminum powder**
West System Epoxy Barrier Additive

**Ammonia**
Armstrong's New Beginnings Extra
Strengh Floor Cleaner
Brasso
Noxon 7
Windex

**Ammonium chloride**
Fantastik

**Anhydrous lanolin**
Lanocote

**Anionic surfactant**
Dreft
Sudbury Boat Zoap

**Aromatic polyisocyanate**
Interlux AL 200 Fiberglass Primer

**Bleach**
Clorox
Soft Scrub with Bleach

**Borax**
20 Mule Team Borax

**Bronopol**
Thetford's Aqua-Kem Holding Tank
Deodorant

**2 Butoxyethanol**
MaryKate Spray Away Cleaner

**Butoxyethanol**
Castrol Super Clean

**Calcium carbonate**
Bon Ami

**Calcium chloride**
MDR Damp Away

**Chlorine**
Clorox
Soft Scrub With Bleach

**Citronella**
Avon's Skin-So-Soft

**Cuprous oxide**
MDR Inflatable and Dinghy Bottom
Coating

**Cyanoacrylate**
3M Quick Fix Adhesive
Pasco-Fix

**Dibasic ester**
Peel Away Marine Safety Strip

**Dimethyl ether**
3M Spray Trim Adhesive

**Ethanol**
Interlux Viny-Lux Primewash 353/354

**Ethyl alcohol**
Rain X

**Ethylene glycol**
Sudbury Bilge Cleaner

**Enzymes**
Microbe-Clean Marine
Dreft
Spray 'n Wash

**Epoxy**
Evercoat Aluminox Epoxy Sticks
Faststeel Steel Reinforced Epoxy Putty
"Git"-Rot
Interlux 417A/418B
Interlux Epoxy Barrierkote 404/414
Interlux Epoxy Fairing and Surfacing
Compound
Interlux Interprotect 1000/1001
Interlux Interprotect 2000/2001
Interlux Interprotect Watertite
V135A/136A
Marine-Tex
Pettit 7020/7025
Pettit Flexbond Marine Epoxy

Polymeric System Epoxy Strip

Polymeric System Quikplastik Epoxy
Putty Plastic Adhesive

Rustoleum Epoxy Concrete Surfacer

West System Epoxy

Woolsey Gold

Woolsey Gold Primer

**Fluoropolymer resin**

303 Fabric Guard

**Formaldehyde**

Thetford's Aqua-Kem Holding Tank
Deodorant

**Glycol**

Pampers Baby Fresh

**Hydrocarbon resin**

Interlux Underwater Primer 360

**Hydrocarbon solvent**

Corrosion X

**Hydrochloric acid**

On & Off

**Hydrogen peroxide**

Clorox 2

**Isobutane**

Endust

Blue Coral Dri-Clean Carpet and
Upholstery Cleaner

**Isocyanate**

Evercoat Urethane Foam

**Isoparaffinic hydrocarbon solvent**

Pledge

**Kerosene**

3M Super Duty Rubbing Compound

**Ketone**

Interlux Fiberglass Solvent Wash 202

**Lanolin**

Forespar Lanocote Corrosion Inhibitor

Lan-Lin

**Linear polyurethane**

Awlgrip

**Methyl alcohol**

Thetford's Aqua-Kem Holding Tank
Deodorant

**Methanol**

Interlux Pintoff 299E

**Methylene chloride**

Interlux AL 200 Fiberglass Primer

Interlux Pintoff 299

**Methyl ethyl ketone (MEK)**

Polymarine Inflatable Boat Patch
Adhesive #3026

VLP Clear Liquid Vinyl Repair

**Mineral oil**

West Marine Head Lube

**Mineral spirits**

Nevr-Dull

**Naphtha**

3M General Purpose Adhesive Cleaner

Collinite's #885 Heavy Duty Paste
Fleetwax

**Naphthenic distillate**

West Marine Head Lube

**Nonionic surfactant**

Sudbury Boat Zoap

**Nylon**

Marelon

**Oils**

Murphy's Oil Soap

**Oleic distillates**

Flitz

**Oxalic acid**

Bar Keepers Friend

BoatLIFE Teak Brite Teak Cleaner

BoatLIFE Fiberglass Powder Cleaner
and Stain Remover

FSR

MaryKate On & Off Hull and Bottom
Cleaner

T. L. Sea Marine Cleanser

Y-10 Stain Absorbent Gel

**Paraffinic petroleum oil**

Endust

**Perchlorethylene**

Liquid Wrench

**Petroleum distillates**

303 Fabric Guard

3M Marine Fiberglass Restorer and Wax

3M Ultra Performance Paste Wax

Boeshield T-9

Brasso

CRC Heavy Duty Corrosion Inhibitor

Flitz

Goo Gone

Interlux ACT

Interlux Bilgekote 863

Interlux Fiberglass Solvent Wash 202
Interlux Micron CSC
Interlux Tri-Lux II
Interlux Ultra-Kote
Liquid Wrench
Penetrol
petroleum jelly
Pettit ACP50
Pettit Trinidad
Sikkens Cetol Marine Finish
Spray 'n Wash
Star brite Plastic Polish/Restorer
Star brite Poly System One
Star brite Premium Marine Polish with
    Teflon
Star brite Waterproofing and Fabric
    Treatment
Vaseline Intensive Care
WD-40 Spray Lubricant
West Marine Boat Polish
Woolsey Neptune

**Phosphate**
West Marine TSP
Ultra Solv

**Phosphoric acid**
naval jelly
Ospho
On & Off

**Polyester**
Evercoat Fiberglass Resin
Evercoat Gel Coat Scratch Patch
Evercoat Premium Gel Paste

**Polyethylene glycol ether derivatives**
Simple Green

**Polyglycol dimethylacrylate**
Loctite #242 Removable Thread Locker

**Polyol**
Evercoat Urethane Foam

**Polyolefin**
Interlux Polymeric Noskid Compound
    2398
Woolsey Non-Skid Compound

**Polysulfide**
BoatLIFE Life Calk
3M Polysulfide Marine Sealant 101

**Polyurethane**
3M Marine Adhesive Sealant Fast Cure
    4200
3M Adhesive Sealant 5200

**Polyurethane/silicone hybrid**
BoatLIFE Life Seal

**Polyurethane varnish**
Epifanes Matte
Interlux Clipper
Pettit Ultra V-Gold

**Polyurethane paint**
Interlux Brightside
Pettit Easypoxy
Woolsey Miracote

**Polyvinyl acetate**
Elmer's Glue

**Polyvinyl butraldehyde**
Interlux Viny-Lux Primewash 353/354

**Potassium hydroxide**
MDR Inflatable Dinghy Cleaner

**Pumice**
Castrol Waterless and Towelless Hand
    Cleaner
Lava Bar Soap

**Rubber**
Evercoat Gasket Maker and Sealer

**Silicone**
3M Marine Grade Mildew Resistant
    Silicone
Apseal
Pledge
RTV Silicone Gasket Compound

**Sodium bicarbonate**
baking soda

**Sodium hydroxide**
Castrol Super Clean
Easy Off
Star brite Sea Safe Teak Cleaner

**Sodium laurate ether sulfate**
Woolite

**Sodium hypochlorite**
Clorox
Soft Scrub
Star brite Sea Safe Teak Cleaner

**Solvents**
- acetone
- gasoline
- kerosene
- lacquer thinner
- mineral spirits
- turpentine
- xylol

**Stoddard's Solvent**
- 3M Super Duty Rubbing Compound

**Styrene butadiene**
- Castrol Waterless and Towelless Hand Cleaner

**Teflon**
- Star brite Premium Marine Polish with Teflon
- West Marine Boat Polish

**Tetrohydrofuran**
- VLP Clear Liquid Vinyl Repair

**Toluene**
- Interlux Pintoff 299E
- Polymarine #2990 Hypalon Adhesive

**Triclosan**
- Joy

**Tung oil**
- Epifanes Gloss Varnish
- Interlux Schooner
- Pettit Easypoxy High-Build

**Turpenes**
- Murphy's Oil Soap
- Murphy's Oil Soap Spray

**Vinyl**
- MDR Liquid Lectric Tape
- West Marine Liquid Electrical Tape

**Vinylester**
- 3M Marine Water-Barrier Coating

**Xylene**
- Interlux Underwater Primer 360

**Zinc chromate**
- Interlux Viny-Lux Primewash 353/354

**Zinc dust**
- CRC Instant Galvanize

**Zinc dialkyl-dithiophosphate**
- STP Oil Treatment

# Product Index

This appendix lists the commercial products and cleaning chemicals mentioned in this book. Following each product name is a description of its primary use. Page numbers indicate where individual products are mentioned in the text.

# Index

# ABOUT THE AUTHOR

Bill Burr has spent a lifetime at sea, sailing and crewing on everything from Sunfish and 45-foot racing boats to 100-foot powerboats. His *Sailing Tips, 1,000 New Ways to Solve Old Problems* has been a popular source for boaters since 1989. Now retired, he approaches boat maintenance and marine products with over 40 years of experience in the chemical industry. In the process of researching this book, he spent a year selling coatings and compounds in a marine store. He currently lives aboard his 37-foot Jeanneau sailboat and every day faces the problems addressed in the book. Like all boaters, he continues looking for new solutions to old maintenance problems.